# The Permissive Morality

# The Permissive Morality

C. H. WHITELEY
M.A., PH.D.
*Reader in Philosophy*
*University of Birmingham*

WINIFRED M. WHITELEY
B.A., M.COMM.

METHUEN & CO LTD
11 NEW FETTER LANE · LONDON EC4

*First published in 1964*

*Printed in Great Britain*
*by Cox & Wyman Ltd*
*London, Fakenham and Reading*

# Contents

Must not such a society take freedom as far as it will go? . . . So fathers behave like children and are afraid of their sons, and children neither respect nor fear their parents, because this is freedom. Teachers are afraid of their pupils and pander to them, and pupils despise their teachers; and in general the young act like their elders and challenge them in word and deed, and the old give way to the young and are very familiar and easy-going, imitating their juniors so that nobody can call them bad-tempered or bossy. . . . But the final plenitude of freedom is reached in this society when hired servants are just as free as their employers. This same freedom and equality appears in the relations between men and women.

Plato, *Republic*, Book VIII.

# Foreword

Like most people of our generation, we have been struck by the change in moral outlook that has taken place since we were children. The object of this book is to try to get a clearer picture of how this change has come about, and what effect it is having on the quality of people's experience.

We have begun by describing some of the more obvious changes in outlook concerning sex, parent–child relationships, treatment of criminals, and individual economic responsibility. In all these we find a common tendency towards increased permissiveness. Among the causes of this tendency we have noted the economic emancipation of women, young people and the working classes, and the increased domination of life by large-scale organizations. Ideas also have played their part. We have discussed the declining influence of religion and its replacement by scientific ways of thinking. In more detail we have examined the growing influence of two groups of people, the psychiatrists and the publicity men. We then inquire what, if anything, contemporary philosophy has to contribute to morality.

In what ways, we ask, is the new morality an improvement on the old, in terms of the ensuing quality of experience? What are its corresponding deficiencies? For we think that something of the meaning and purpose of life has been lost – life has become flatter and more aimless. Some look to education to remedy this lack in contemporary life. Others try to find in leisure activities the satisfaction missing from their working lives. We have tried to judge what can be hoped for from each of these resources, and conclude with a glimpse into the possible future.

We do not claim to present new information, since we refer only to such facts as we believe to be familiar enough not to require statistical evidence. Our aim is philosophical (in the original sense of the term): to achieve a comprehensive view of the contemporary moral attitude and its sources, and to comment on its strengths and weaknesses.

# I · Changes in Morality since 1900

Most people would agree that there have been important changes in the moral standards of the English over the past sixty years. But what exactly does this mean? What constitutes the moral standards of a people, or of an individual?

If one judges a man's standards by what he professes, one risks being misled. For some men are hypocrites who preach what they make no effort to practise, whereas others are too diffident or too scrupulous to profess higher standards than they manage to achieve. So to compare the morality of our grandparents as a group with that of our contemporaries by examining what both have openly professed in sermons, leading articles and political manifestos, or on school speech-days and other self-conscious occasions, could easily produce a false impression and would very likely be unfair to our own generation. For we seem to be altogether more sceptical than our grandparents about the declarations of moral principle made by politicians, churchmen, publicists and our own neighbours, and shyer about making such declarations ourselves. This need not mean that we take the principles less seriously, only that we have less confidence in verbal professions of faith as indications of genuine good intent.

But if, on the other hand, one judges a man's standards by his actual behaviour, one risks being misled in other ways.

It is possible to have genuine moral convictions and aspirations and make genuine moral efforts, and yet quite often fail to live up to one's standards. If Jones tells lies or gets drunk somewhat oftener than Brown, this need not mean that Jones has a smaller regard for veracity or sobriety; it may mean that he is more often in situations where it is difficult to speak the truth or to refuse another drink. So the increase in illegitimate births and the decrease in suicides which usually accompany the outbreak of war need not be taken as marking a change in attitudes to the relevant moral rules, but merely in the strength of the temptations to break them. The current increase in law-breaking cannot safely be taken to imply that the average Englishman's respect for his neighbour's rights is less than it was. There are other possible explanations – for instance, that would-be law-breakers now have less fear of being caught and made to suffer.

The best indication of an individual's standards is neither what he does nor what he says that he and other people ought to do, but what he is ashamed and what he is proud of having done or not done. The best indication of the moral standards of a community is the way that community distributes punishment and reward, praise and censure. If there is a kind of action which a man cannot leave undone without incurring disgrace and the loss of friends, of job or advancement, this action counts as an obligation by the standards of the community. And if there is a kind of action which a man cannot perform without suffering similar penalties, this action counts as wrong by the community's standards. Thus we shall reckon that standards have changed in English society wherever we see evidence that things can now be done or omitted with social impunity which, if done or omitted sixty years ago, would have involved damage to reputation, prospects and social status.

The standards we are thinking of are mainly those of the English middle classes, taking this expression in its widest possible sense in which it covers a sizeable part of the more prosperous working classes. In so far as the very rich and powerful on the one hand, and the poorest groups on the other, have had special moral outlooks of their own, we are not so much concerned with them. This is not merely because it is the middle-class standards with which we are ourselves most familiar, but, more importantly, because it is these standards which have mattered most in setting the general tone and pattern of the life of the country.

That changes in these moral standards have taken place cannot be exactly demonstrated either by quoting pronouncements or by analysing statistics, though both these kinds of evidence are relevant. It cannot indeed be exactly demonstrated at all. But it can be a matter of knowledge to anyone who has lived through such a change. For anyone who has to live in a community must be well aware what that community's moral standards are; he has to know what sorts of actions and omissions will get him into trouble and what he can safely get away with. Indeed, if people were not well aware of this, social discipline could not function. So any change in moral standards must be a matter of common knowledge to those who have lived through it.

It seems to us that there have been obvious changes of standards in at least five departments of conduct. Let us begin by taking note of these changes.

The most striking and perhaps the most important change is in sexual morality. In 1900 sex was an unmentionable topic in mixed company with any pretensions to respectability. No description of sexual intercourse was allowed to appear in print, and open allusions to sex were excised from Shakespeare and other literary classics. No schoolmistress dared refer to the topic in front of a class of girls, and plenty of parents refused to say anything about it to their children of either sex. Menstruation came as a shock, and the wedding night as an entire surprise, to great numbers of girls. In 1900 to be divorced counted as a disgrace, a severe handicap in social life and in business, especially if one had been divorced for adultery. A young woman who was known to have lost her virginity stood little chance of making an acceptable marriage.

By contrast, in 1964, sexual matters are freely discussed in almost all kinds of society; sexual intercourse and sexual perversions are not merely referred to but described in print; and the Marriage Guidance Council sends its representatives into the schools to give lectures and conduct discussions on sexual topics with boys and girls. To be divorced, even for adultery, is no longer a serious obstacle to entering the most respectable society, and in very few careers does it impose any handicap. Nor is it now difficult for an unchaste young woman to make a satisfactory match. It is true, young men are apt to express a preference for marrying virgins; but it seems clear that plenty of them are prepared to waive this preference when it comes to the point. It is not of course possible to produce statistical proof that there is much more pre-marital sexual intercourse than there used to be, though this seems very likely. What is quite clear is that no serious attempt is made to prevent girls from going to bed with their boy friends if they want to, nor do any serious penalties follow if they are found out, provided that they have evaded pregnancy. Given the ready availability of contraceptives, the only effective means of securing the chastity of young unmarried people is constant supervision. Whatever the views of present-day parents about pre-marital chastity, they are not sufficiently in earnest to provide this constant supervision, as their grandparents did. Perhaps many of them would like to but dare not, for fear of forfeiting the affection of their children and incurring the deadly reproach of being out of date.

A second change is in the relation between parents and children. Of course, there are very strict and very easy-going parents in every generation; the kind and amount of obedience demanded from children and the means by which it is enforced always vary from one family to another, and there is no such thing as a standard practice. The differences between the generations are in the *proportion* of parents adopting one attitude or another. Certainly the proportion of parents taking the line that children should be seen and not heard has fallen very much since the beginning of the century. Then it was usual for children to have little pocket money and few possessions; to be required (especially if they were girls) to do a number of household tasks; to be given the impression that their first duty was obedience and that disobedience was intolerable to their parents. It was unusual for them to be consulted in any way about the clothes they should wear, the outings on which they should be taken or even the toys to be bought for them. It was very unusual for any kind of cheek, answering back or criticism of the parents' decisions and actions to be allowed to pass unpunished. The child was clearly a subordinate and unprivileged member of the household.

Today it is common for the child to figure as an influential member of the establishment and not so very rare for him to dominate it. The bad boy of the past ran away from his parents; the bad boy of today intimidates them. Children have more money and more possessions. They have a larger voice in choosing their own activities and a greater latitude in doing and saying what they please. They are less likely to be called on for domestic duties. They expect and demand many things from their parents as of right. And they can often express without penalty their disagreement, disapproval or dislike of their parents' characters and behaviour.

A third change is in attitudes to individual economic responsibility. In 1900 the business of providing against sickness, injury, unemployment, old age or bad trade was the responsibility of each individual head of the household, whether he did it by his private savings or through an insurance company or Friendly Society. Nowadays this provision has become predominantly a public responsibility. Medical treatment and sickness benefits, pensions for the aged, the widowed and the disabled, payments to those out of work, are provided from public funds, that is from the pockets of those who are for the time being in good health, of working age and in employment. This acceptance of public responsibility for private hardships was introduced against strong opposition on grounds of principle – the principle that it is the duty and the privilege of each citizen to order his own economic affairs, and that it is not the duty of the community at large to take over these responsibilities, nor is it fair to call upon efficient and provident citizens to subsidize the inefficient and improvident. Principles of this kind were commonly put forward in 1900; they are rarely heard of today.

Such things as school milk and meals, housing subsidies and subsidized rents, and grants for higher education, go even further than the relief of distress, towards trying to ensure for everyone a reasonable level of prosperity and opportunity for the development of talent. If a man cannot easily afford to rent himself a house, or pay a lawyer to conduct a lawsuit for him, we think it proper for the rest of the citizens to be taxed to help him out. Thus both the principle of compulsory universal insurance against misfortune and the principle that the economically strong should aid the economically weak are now accepted by all shades of opinion. Nor is it only the poor who have formed the habit of looking to public authorities to safeguard their standard of living. If an industry becomes less profitable than it was, it is at once assumed that the government should do something to save the investors from loss.

The fourth area of moral change that we shall notice is comparatively unimportant, yet it plays its part in determining the social atmosphere of our day. It is the decline of interest in decorum and ceremony. Sixty years ago much more was made of appropriate formalities for particular occasions. Most such conventions originated among the upper classes, and the lower classes imitated them as best they could. There were rules about what was to be worn at dinner, at the theatre, for mourning, for country walks, in church, in the lecture room. There were proper forms of address, proper and improper words and topics of conversation in a given type of company. Respectable women did not smoke or swear in public. Among the more prosperous working class there was the wearing of "Sunday best" and the loving maintenance of the "front room" furnished as expensively as the family could manage and used only on important social occasions. Except in the family and among intimate friends, first names were not commonly used. There was a marked distinction between the language of ordinary conversation and the stiffer and more ornate language of literature and public speaking.

But today formality is shunned (except perhaps at weddings where it still persists, even among people who have to consult a book of etiquette to find out what should be done and worn). Evening dress is dying out. In our own university the wearing of gowns for lectures stopped during the war and has not been resumed, and many junior lecturers call their professor by his first name. Swearing has become a matter of personal taste. We all buy our shirts from the same chain-store. Politicians give fireside chats, and philosophers try to write technical treatises in the language of the man on the Clapham bus. If on some rare occasion one wants to show respect to somebody, one hardly knows how to set about it, because the formal procedures are obsolete.

Finally, there has been a change in our moral attitudes towards crime and criminals. There are two points of view from which criminals can be regarded. According to the first, people commit crimes because they are wicked; they could refrain from crime if they tried hard enough, and the purpose of punishment is to make them try. According to the second point of view, criminals are people who by reason of their hereditary constitution and the influence of their environment are abnormally prone to anti-social activities. When one understands all the circumstances, one sees that they were bound to act as they did. Punishment should therefore be combined with or replaced by some attempt to refashion their personalities so that their inclinations to commit crime are diminished.

During the period under consideration the second point of view has gained much ground as against the first. Probation, introduced in 1907, has come to replace punishment for large numbers of offenders. In the actual punishments there is less of retribution and more of reformation; corporal punishment has been abolished, except in prisons, capital punishment has become extremely rare, and "corrective training" and "preventive detention" have made their appearance. Juvenile offenders are handled separately from adults and the sentences they receive are aimed at retraining them rather than at making them suffer. The mentally defective or mentally disturbed offender can now be sent for treatment instead of punishment; the "psychopathic" criminal is recognized as a distinct type requiring different handling, and mental disorder is accepted as diminishing criminal responsibility. In all these ways the straightforward connection between guilt and penalty is modified by attempts to re-adjust the characters of criminals.

These five kinds of change in current moral standards have not coincided by accident: they fit together and form parts of one coherent pattern. They express in different ways a single comprehensive modification in our attitude to human life and human morality. If the change is to be put into a few words, it can be described as a general relaxation of standards, a greater permissiveness, a raising of the demands a man may make on life and a lowering of the demands life can make on him. We may elaborate this by sketching two extreme views of life and morality.

On the first view, life is seen as a task to be accomplished, a challenge to achievement. Success in it will involve attaining certain standards, obeying certain rules. These rules and standards are not devised by men – they may be thought of as devised by God, or as inherent in the nature of things. It is not very difficult to recognize these standards; anyone of normal understanding and adequate sincerity should be able to tell the difference between moral right and wrong, and no very special gifts are needed to distinguish sound from shoddy craftsmanship, or good from bad works of art. The difficulty lies not in recognizing the standards, but in obeying them, and this calls for the exercise of strength of will. The difference between the good and successful man, who achieves the standards, and the bad and unsuccessful man who does not, is held to be mainly a matter of moral effort. Of course not everybody can be first-rate at his job. But everybody can reach an adequate standard of honesty, industry, decency and consideration for others. If he fails to do so he cannot have been trying hard enough: he is to blame and must strive to improve his performance. If he succeeds he has earned the right to be happy, for happiness is the reward of virtue, attained only after it has been deserved. Some people have maintained the even stronger alternative view that the practice of virtue is itself happiness. What comes by luck or cheating or someone else's charity cannot be genuine happiness; it is somehow tainted, and will not give real satisfaction. Every man bears the responsibility for his own prosperity in this life and his salvation in the next; not to accept this responsibility, not to pay your way, is a disgrace. The leading ideas of this philosophy of life (on which we and most of our contemporaries were brought up) are the ideas of a task to be accomplished, universal rules to be obeyed, personal responsibility for success or failure, and satisfaction as the due reward of effort.

On the second view, commoner today, life is seen in terms of the pursuit of happiness or satisfaction. It is assumed that everyone has a right to be happy, and all laws and institutions should be devised so as to promote the greatest happiness of the greatest number. In living we aim constantly at satisfying the various natural desires that we all have and all should be able to fulfil; therefore to impair another man's chances of fulfilling his desires is to do him a grave wrong. There is nothing so bad as frustration, and if many people suffer from it there is something amiss with the society they live in, something which should be detected and put right. Thus responsibility for a man's happiness falls not on himself alone, but also on society at large, and especially on those in power. Again, if he fails to live up to accepted standards of behaviour, this will not be due to himself only; it will result from the interplay of his innate and acquired tendencies with his environment, and since he did not choose his innate tendencies, nor his parents and their manner of bringing him up, nor the main features of his present environment, we cannot throw the whole blame for his errors and failings upon him. He does not have to show cause why he should be happy, producing evidence that he has earned his happiness before being allowed to enjoy it; on the contrary, society needs to show cause why he should be miserable before his misery can be reckoned allowable. On this view there are no universal moral standards applicable to everyone; moral rules and standards are only conventionally accepted devices for securing co-operation and avoiding conflict – they are the concessions that each individual has to make in the pursuit of his own satisfactions to enable other individuals to pursue their satisfactions too. As to the right manner of life and the right course of conduct, these will vary under differing material and social conditions, and for individuals of differing temperaments and capacities. So it is not easy to know what is the most desirable way to live, even for oneself. This has to be discovered by trial and error, and there is room for moral experiment and for the exercise of choice. Any moral rule which obstructs opportunities for people to enjoy themselves inoffensively should be scrapped or modified. Thus morality is not primary and central in human life, but marginal and instrumental.

On the first view, morality is self-justifying, and claims to happiness are justified by good behaviour. On the second view, it is happiness that is self-justifying, and morality is justified by the contribution it makes to happiness.

Here are two contrasted points of view, each providing a coherent approach to the business of living. And each of the changes we have mentioned is away from a manner of life consistent with the first, and towards a manner of life consistent with the second.

# II · Parallel Changes in the Arts

This increased permissiveness, this tendency towards the relaxation of standards, which we have noticed in many of our moral attitudes, has appeared during the same period in the theory and practice of the fine arts. Most ages, indeed, have had their innovators and their modernist movements, setting up new aims, new canons of excellence in opposition to the customary. But the twentieth century is peculiar in having produced artistic movements in which all need for canons or standards of any kind is denied. This is most evident in painting and sculpture.

Previous European schools of painting agreed in regarding their art as a means to the representation of some aspect of the nature of things. They differed in the kind and degree of truth-to-nature that was demanded. Some chose to represent the structure, colour and texture of material things; others the facts and significance of momentous events; others the visible expression of personality or emotion. But all of them subjected themselves to the discipline of portraying some object in terms of a particular pictorial language, having its own rules. Once the observer understood what the artist had in mind and what were the conventions of his method of portrayal, he could judge whether the work succeeded or failed.

But the contemporary observer, presented with a gallery full of modern abstracts, is helpless to judge them, not because he is unfamiliar with their canons, but because there are no canons. This kind of painting admits no rules of composition, no pictorial conventions, no discipline. There is no test of success and failure except whether or not the painting gives this particular spectator some sort of thrill. And this rejection of discipline is deliberate. It is justified by aesthetic theories in which the main function of a work of art is to provide an expression for the feelings of the artist. He is to paint without thought of any object to be represented, without thought of any public to whom his work is to be made intelligible, just trying to present his emotions on the canvas in whatever way seems suitable to himself.[1] The artistic movement which produced Futurism, Surrealism and their successors is described by Sir Herbert Read as "not a revolution but a dissolution". It involves a rejection of standards, and of the whole idea of the artistic endeavour as a task governed by rules of right and wrong; it expresses the demand for satisfaction of the artist's impulses as a good thing in itself, justifiable *per se*. This point of view is exemplified more extravagantly in the arts than in other human activities, since standardless spontaneity is a possible method of artistic production, but

[1] Compare these statements:

"Any imitation of nature, however concealed, is a lie." (Archipenko.)

"The inner element, i.e. the emotion, determines the form of the work of art." (Kandinsky.)

"Pure psychic automatism, by which it is intended to express the real process of thought . . . free from any control by the reason, independent of any aesthetic or moral preoccupation." (Breton.)

"The big moment came when it was decided to paint . . . just TO PAINT. The gesture on the canvas was a gesture of liberation from Value – political, aesthetic, moral." (H. Rosenberg.)

not a possible approach where more utilitarian activities are concerned.

Partly for this reason, the extremism appearing in painting and sculpture cannot be matched in other arts. Buildings have to be stable and functional, and literature must achieve at least some degree of intelligibility. Nevertheless the other arts have displayed similar trends. The abandonment of tonality in music was an upheaval comparable to the abandonment of representation in painting and took place around the same time; and some later music seems to consist of irregular successions of bangs and squeaks lacking all organized form. In literature, we have had a rejection of the discipline of rhyme and metre, and a number of attempts to cross the boundaries of conventional grammar and vocabulary, and more recently such exercises in formlessness and pointlessness as Samuel Beckett's plays, which the author describes as "the expression that there is nothing to express".

Only a part of modern art belongs to or is much influenced by movements of this kind. But their very existence marks a frame of mind peculiar to the twentieth century. Wherever they prevail, their effect is to isolate the artist from the rest of the community. Rejecting the discipline of conventional standards, rejecting the obligation to be intelligible, he produces only for the attention of small coteries and cliques, those few who are close enough students of his manner to understand what he is about, or so determined to be "advanced" that they pretend to understand. Of the rest of us, those who are appreciative of high art, but not able to make this a full-time occupation, are for the most part driven back on the masterpieces of past generations. Now that easy travel has opened to us the picture galleries of all Europe, and the radio and gramophone bring the world's leading orchestras into our sitting rooms, we get on well enough without making the inordinate effort needed to come to terms with modernist extravagances. But a much larger audience is catered for by a modern art of a very different kind – the "popular" commercial entertainment art which is deliberately aimed at the aesthetically insensitive and undeveloped and deliberately tries to be superficial and ephemeral. So some of the ablest and most devoted artists lose contact with the general public. There is more here than the usual time-lag between artistic originality and common taste. There is a loss of the contribution artists might make towards sharpening our vision and deepening our sympathies. Too often, the ordinary person receives instead from contemporary art a sensation of disorientation and bewilderment.

# III · The Social Background

Moral principles may be thought of as the attempts of men living in communities to find satisfactory patterns of behaviour for dealing with the situations that confront them. As these social situations change, so men change their minds about the best moral rules for dealing with them. It may be presumed that the alterations in our moral principles are connected with the different situations which our contemporaries have to meet by contrast with their grandparents. We will now try to trace some of the differences of social and economic situation which have influenced and continue to influence the moral changes.

The past sixty years have been marked by a general trend towards reducing inequalities in power and privilege. Groups of people formerly in subordinate positions have achieved greater independence and a greater opportunity of influencing the common standards. In particular, women have come to occupy a stronger position relatively to men, children relatively to adults, and the working classes relatively to other economic classes. All these changes have contributed to altering moral standards in the ways we have been considering.

One effect of the emancipation of women is seen in the field of sexual morality. Chastity used to be a virtue imposed on women by their husbands or prospective husbands. (Men did not impose it with the same stringency on themselves, except that each man kept the others away from his own woman.)

It was enforced by male economic domination, and where that domination still exists, chastity can still be enforced. But the present-day woman enjoys a large measure of economic independence. She is not compelled to find some man who will support her in order to gain a livelihood; she can get a job and support herself. And being her own mistress she can please herself as regards her sexual behaviour. Quite often she does not please to wait for sexual gratification until she has managed to acquire a husband, nor does she remain faithful to a husband who no longer satisfies her if she can transfer herself with her property or earning power to another man whom she likes better.

A further effect of the independent employment of women is that the married woman who goes out to work has a slacker disciplinary grip on her children. Often away from home, and too tired when she is at home to expend much effort on the training of her offspring, she is apt to leave them to their own devices or trust the schoolmistress to do this part of her job for her.

The effects of the emancipation of children are if anything even more far-reaching. Once again this is partly based on economic circumstances. The juvenile just leaving school finds himself able to command an income sufficient to give him some measure of independence at home, and purchasing power in the market. He does not work under his father's direction, and very rarely depends on his father's influence or recommendation in getting his job. He has a great deal more free time than in the past and a great many more resources to employ in it outside the family circle along with associates of his own age; especially, the size of modern urban communities and the availability of motor transport take him very quickly out of sight and earshot of neighbours as well as parents.

The economic factor is reinforced by others which weaken parental control. In a more traditional and ignorant community, parents are people of superior knowledge and experience, regarded by the young with respect, whether admiring or grudging. But in present-day society how little father and mother seem to know in comparison with all the professional talkers! Schoolmasters soon take the pupil beyond the point where his parents could help with his homework; radio and television bring into the family's own sitting-room an endless succession of strangers wiser, more glamorous and seductive, with more stimulating notions and more exciting experiences than Mum or Dad. As Dad cannot compete with the experts who instruct, so Mum cannot compete with the efficient and charming synthetic housewives who appear in the advertisements. In a world so full of specialist talent, so openly displayed, one's own family inevitably appears very small beer. In a world in which everything changes so fast, parental wisdom seems already out of date, and not worth a lively young fellow's attention. Some years ago the parents' way of life was the principal model for that of the children, but today it is not so. Young people look forward to a life far more opulent, free and varied than that of their parents. The style of living in which they were raised becomes something to escape from or improve on, the point of view of their elders something to be superseded in the necessary progress of human affairs. The word "square" is the symbol of this attitude, which is often adopted towards teachers too, whenever these do nothing but purvey education of a traditional kind, lacking in obvious relevance to the occupations and problems of the workaday world. Such teachers often fail to inspire in their pupils any respect for either their subject matter, themselves or the values they extol. The young people are convinced that their own role is to confront life unhampered by what seem to them to be out-of-date prejudices. (The point of view of the exceptional young people in H. G. Wells's novels has now become normal.) Moreover, they have good reason to be even less patient than young people commonly have been. For what if there should be no future after all? The consciousness of this danger, more acute in the young than in their elders, makes them more impatient to please themselves while there is still time; it increases their resentment against the older generation that has wandered to the brink of the precipice.

This increased independence of young people in its turn weakens the confidence of parents in their claims to their children's obedience and respect. Sexual laxity also is in part a consequence of the opportunities young people have to flout their parents' sexual standards without risk of discovery (the motor-car is an important factor here) and without fear of effective reprisals.

But one can go further than this, and suggest that the whole standpoint of our society tends more and more to be a juvenile standpoint – impatient, improvident, indecorous and disrespectful, avid for novelty and variety. Teenagers (the neologism "teenager" is itself significant of the recognition of a new social class) have become more important buyers of goods and especially of entertainment; the cinema industry now depends principally on the custom of adolescents, and adolescent "stars" in substantial numbers appear for the first time in history upon our stages. So the teenage image and values are more insistently pressed upon our attention and offered for our imitation. Middle-aged women dress in short tight skirts and hobble around in winkle-picker shoes because the fashions are adapted to the tastes and physiques of the young girls who dominate the market. So the manner of behaviour which appeals to the young comes to seem a normal standard for the whole community.

One element in this manner of behaviour seems to be a greater propensity to law-breaking. An increase in delinquency, predominantly juvenile delinquency, is a feature of modern life not only in Britain but throughout those countries (including some little affected by the war) which are caught up in the same advance of affluence, mass production, urbanization and mobility. No doubt the causes of delinquency are extremely complex;[1] but the principal cause of this recent expansion of juvenile crime is, we suggest, the emancipation of young people from effective adult control. The behaviour of contemporary working-class gangs is quite similar to that of groups of upper-class undergraduate hooligans in the past, who also had leisure, resources, freedom from adult control, and no fear of destitution.

As to the enhanced status and influence of the working classes, its effects are seen in other ways. One is the decline of decorum and the growth of informality. Formality is usually valued by ruling groups rather than by those ruled. Special sorts of dress for particular occasions, special manners of speech, special modes of courtesy, are cultivated by people who can spare the time and the money to elaborate their transactions in this fashion, and so mark themselves off from the vulgar mob who have not acquired such graces and do not know the proper thing to do. By contrast, the proletarian reckons mateyness as one of the prime values, and dislikes and distrusts anyone who puts on airs. In this respect the English people as a whole have gone over to the proletarian standpoint and are all trying hard to be just ordinary chaps. (The resolute affability of titled persons showing crowds

[1] See T. R. Fyvel, *The Insecure Offenders*.

of sightseers over their stately homes provides some nice examples.)

Again, there is the changed attitude to social responsibility for individual welfare. The idea that a man should be solely and individually responsible for his own success in life never appealed very much to the working man. How could it? He could see only too well that his prosperity was very much at the mercy of the arbitrary decisions of bosses, of the unforeseeable and uncontrollable vagaries of economic supply and demand, and of the random visitations of disease and accident which could make a mockery of his attempts to provide for his own future. The wage-worker cannot organize his own working life and secure his own prosperity. So he wants things organized by the governing authorities to safeguard the welfare of himself and his mates. He wants a joint effort at joint prosperity, and he puts security well ahead of progress. In this respect also we are, as a nation, much more proletarian than we were.

Thirdly, it is generally held that, though there were a good many harsh and violent working-class fathers, the middle classes used to discipline their children with a more effective strictness than did the working classes. In so far as we are relaxing our control over our children, we are taking the back-street Mum as our model instead of the bourgeois Mamma.

Besides these respects in which the middle classes are becoming more proletarian, there are others in which the working classes are becoming more bourgeois. The most important is that a rising standard of living has become an accepted aim, and the house, the car, the annual holiday and the children's scholastic record become items in a competitive display between a family and its neighbours. The difference in outlook between the classes is diminishing in modern mass society, though it has by no means disappeared.

For while the proletariat is improving its status, the middle class is at the same time changing its character, and this change is very important for the shift in moral standards that we are concerned with. The old morality of strict standards and little mercy for those who failed to live up to them, the morality of self-control, of postponing satisfactions until they had been earned, the vision of life as a challenging task with a reward at the end if it was properly done – this morality was modelled on the economic life of the independent middle-class man, the small business man, the shopkeeper, the free-lance craftsman or doctor or writer or inventor. He worked in and for his own business, he could feel that his success or failure depended mainly on his own talent and application. He saved money now in the reasonable hope of drawing larger dividends later; he thought in terms of investment and returns, and saw that in order to do well he would have to be provident, self-controlled, self-reliant. He was oriented to achievement rather than enjoyment. He had to be his own conscientious supervisor and keep himself up to scratch because he had no master to do it for him. He found his working life interesting because he was his own boss, and because in the economic conditions of his period he saw a reasonable hope of ending his career a good deal better off than when he started – as well as a reasonable fear of bankruptcy if he didn't keep his nose to the grindstone. This is the kind of life-experience that produces the rather Puritan morality which now appears to be declining.

Now this kind of life-experience is becoming much rarer. Nearly everybody is an employee, a servant of some corporation or other. A man's prosperity no longer depends merely on a combination of his effort and his luck. It depends also on the prosperity of the firm and his own ability to keep on good terms with his immediate superiors. His wage or salary is probably fixed by some national agreement between an employers' association and a trade union or professional association, and is to a large extent independent of the quality of the work he does. On the job, he follows instructions; somebody else decides for him what he shall do and how, when, where, with what tools and by what methods he shall do it. The employee who tried to exercise independent judgement would merely dislocate the organization. Mass production means that every action has to be exactly routinized, every individual's performance fitted into everyone else's. Even with the more intellectual forms of labour, even with those forms people are apt to call "creative", the case today is not so very different. The managers of industry, the scientific researchers, the writers of film scripts, are all members of teams, by contrast with their nineteenth-century equivalents, who worked on their own. The plans are made, the results achieved, by collective ingenuity and collective decision, and the glory and the responsibility are collective too.

The same sort of change is taking place with many family responsibilities. There was a time when a man and his wife were fully responsible for bringing up their children, getting them educated, settling them in a job or a career. But now, the children are in school from the age of five or less – as soon, indeed, as the mother can get them off her hands and be released to earn. When they leave school, the employment exchanges are there to find them jobs. They are quickly independent enough to forget what their parents have told them and go their own ways. Similarly, people used to be responsible for taking care of their aged parents – there was a nexus of mutual service and responsibility within the family circle. But now, support for the aged, as for the sick, is provided out of public and not private funds; and increasingly, within the limitations set by inadequate supply of "beds", they are cared for in institutions instead of at home. In the past, probably the most strongly emphasized Christian duty was charity to those worse off than oneself. But the relief of the indigent is now an organized affair, in which individuals have no say. A man can make his contribution to the Refugee Year collection, but what happens to the refugees does not much depend on his or anybody's contribution; it depends on whether there are governments prepared to accept these refugees and give them a place to live in and a job to do – and this is a collective decision.

As for political decisions themselves, they seem by their intricate and technical character to recede further and further beyond the reach of the ordinary citizen (even if one ignores the increasing extent to which his own government is affected in its decisions by the need to reach agreement with other governments – sometimes, a novelty for England, more powerful governments). And local politics, where an individual might expect to find more scope for his personal knowledge and judgement, is as completely as national politics under the domination of the party machine, so that whoever does not faithfully toe the party line is ejected from the scene. In all these ways individual decision and individual responsibility are being superseded by decisions and responsibilities which are impersonal and collective.

We may notice two important ways in which this new situation affects our moral standpoint. Firstly, in a world in which economic self-reliance is no longer a likely way to individual prosperity or even a source of communal prosperity, self-reliance ceases to be seen as a virtue. There is no virtue in thrift when the savings required to keep the economy moving are made by mammoth firms out of their profits and by governments out of taxation, so that the individual's voluntary contributions are of small import. His part in the process is to spend and so keep up the high level of demand by which prosperity seems to be maintained! There is no virtue in self-help when collective provision for needs is so much more effective and economical – national insurance looks after unemployment and old age far better than personal savings could ever do; national schools and universities with scholarships for the bright students to attend them do far more than private enterprise could even attempt; one nursery-school teacher can look after a roomful of toddlers, and do it with professional skill and concern, releasing all their mothers from the nuisance of a child about the house, for ever impeding the woman from getting on with her various tasks.

Secondly, to the extent that relations with and obligations to individuals are replaced by relations with and obligations to corporations, the sense of obligation itself loses much of its force and urgency. Obligations to individuals make an impact on our emotions. Put a man in an intimate face-to-face relationship with another, and he will feel a compunction about hurting that other in his fortune or feelings. But where his obligations are to corporations, there is no such emotional impact. A man who would indignantly resent the suggestion that he might pinch something from his mate's pocket will think nothing of scrounging valuable property from the works. Diddling the income-tax or the customs has never been regarded as a wrong of the same order as diddling an individual customer or creditor. In the bad old days of moneyed privilege, if a young fellow of high intelligence had been enabled to get a university education through the generosity of a local man of means or a committee of relatives and friends who had put up the money, he would have felt obliged to put himself out to do them some service in return when he had got his degree and become launched on his career. But now, when all the citizens club together to pay for the brighter young people to get their university training, these feel no sense of obligation to the impersonal public authority which has mechanically taken care of them. On the contrary, they queue up for tickets to take them across the Atlantic where the rewards seem to be greater. Of course, systematic organization gets immensely more students into Universities; but like any other kind of elaborate organization it makes the whole process automatic and drains it of any moral or sentimental content. If you cheat your neighbour, you see him, or can imagine him, being upset, having to go without something he could otherwise have had; there is something here to stir your compassion. But if you manage to ride first-class on a second-class ticket, or get a job abroad after being trained here at public expense, nobody suffers any loss, nobody is upset, and the total damage to any one person affected has to be reckoned in millionths of a penny. What is there to cause you any compunction?

Further, ordinary ideas of moral responsibility do not easily fit into a situation in which life is dominated by corporate decisions. It seems reasonable to hold a man responsible only for what he knowingly and willingly does. But how is one to apply this principle to actions which are essentially corporate? So many of the things we do are things which nobody decides on and nobody could decide on by himself. The question "Who is responsible?" fails to get an answer. How far was the ordinary German citizen responsible for Belsen and Buchenwald? the ordinary Conservative voter for Suez? How far is a salesman responsible for the quality of the firm's goods? a professor in Johannesburg for educational apartheid? a research scientist for his government's application of his discoveries to prepare for atomic or bacteriological warfare? So much of our lives is dominated by collective decisions, so full is our world of actions which are nobody's in particular and for which nobody in particular is responsible, that there is a loss of contact between a man's personality and principles on the one hand, and his corporately directed activities on the other; what he perforce does is not the outcome of what he is and believes. Consider, as an extreme but characteristic case, the position of the conscientious objector in wartime. If a man does not approve of the war his community is waging with its full forces, what can he do? A century ago he could keep out of it by refusing either to fight in it or to do anything contributing to the waging of it. But this is impossible now that war is total. The critic of pacifism during the last war could say correctly that any job an objector did was indirectly assisting the country's total military effort – helping to support those who were fighting or making weapons, releasing another man or woman for more directly military service. In a state of total mobilization there is no entirely neutral occupation. Similarly with the problem of collaboration in occupied countries. Everybody not actually on the run in the maquis was of necessity a collaborator; the differences were only of degree. (It is not being suggested that differences of degree cannot be extremely important; the difference between child and adult is a difference of degree.) So every citizen of a modern more-or-less totalitarian state who is not actually breaking the laws is a collaborator with the social system and the purposes of the government, however little he approves of them. He cannot escape this collaboration; if he tries to retire into a hermitage, he will probably discover that the likeliest sites have been taken over by the War Office. It has been observed that the perpetrators of Nazi atrocities in concentration camps and elsewhere were often people of averagely humane conduct in their private lives. But this personal character was without effect on their impersonal official actions; these actions being directed by an authority which they could not effectively oppose, they came to feel that the evil they did was inevitable, and that they were not personally responsible for it.

Thus the whole philosophy of living based on the idea that happiness is a reward of effort – individual effort – comes to seem out of place in a world in which most effort is collective, and what comes to a man depends mostly on the efforts of other people and the dispositions of the Organization. And the sense of moral responsibility itself, the idea that a man is obliged to make the best that can be made of his life, and is somehow answerable for what he does with it, this sense which is at the heart of moral endeavour can hardly fail to diminish in intensity. It is not merely the feeling of obligation to corporations, it is the general feeling of responsibility before the task of living, that is impaired by the super-organized society in which we live.

These are obvious ways in which the economic emancipation of women, young people and the working classes as a whole have affected the moral outlook of our society, making for increased permissiveness in sexual relations and the training of children, and reinforcing the tendency of large-scale organization in every field to release the individual from his personal responsibilities. There may well be other causal connections between social changes and the development of the new permissive morality which readers can detect for themselves.

# IV · The Decline of Religion and the Rise of Science

Alongside the changed circumstances of life which we have been reviewing, there are changes in ideas and theories affecting our moral standards. The dominant theories of human life are different at the present time from what they were in our grandparents' day, and authority and leadership in ideas are exercised by different sets of people.

The most conspicuous of these changes is a weakening of the moral authority of the churches and of Christian doctrine.[1] A decline in church membership and church observance over the period we are concerned with is obvious: participation in services and other church activities is a rarer thing among English people in this generation than it was sixty years ago, and very likely rarer than at any time since the country became officially Christian. It is not quite so easy to see how far the decline in church attendance means a decline in Christian belief and outlook. No doubt, many of those who went to church in our grandparents' time went for the sake of convention, and took little heed of what was said and done there. And no doubt, many of our contemporaries who do not go to church retain some essential Christian beliefs and moral principles. Yet, when all allowances have been made, there cannot be much doubt

[1] Most of what we say in this chapter is intended to apply with at least equal force to attendance at synagogues and Jewish doctrine.

that Christian ways of thinking fill a smaller part in the lives of this generation than of its predecessors.

If a man is a member of a church or chapel, attending its services and meetings, making friends with other members, taking his recreation under its auspices, being visited by its minister, reading its literature, paying out of his own pocket to maintain it, he is likely to conform to a pattern of behaving and thinking which is characteristic of that religious group. When he comes up against a moral issue, he tackles it in terms of his religion's teaching, with something of the feeling of his fellow-members looking over his shoulder to see how he copes with it; and when he acts, he does so under the observant eyes of the congregation. A church has a doctrine about the will of God, and a customary style of interpreting that will, a customary set of emphases on virtues to be sought and vices to be avoided, worked out in the regular discussion of moral problems, and thus it forms the consciences of its members. This influence is felt by insincere and half-hearted members as well as by devotees. No such influence affects the person who still professes Christian principles, but whose only contact with organized Christianity is to listen to an occasional broadcast sermon.

In effect, moral issues are now very rarely discussed in terms of the Christian concepts of divine law, sin, Christian charity, and what is necessary to salvation. During a long experience of ethical discussions with University students and a variety of adult education classes, while we have met people (mostly Catholics) who based their morality on ecclesiastical authority, we have found scarcely anyone who tried to settle a disputed point by reference to a matter of religious doctrine, or by quoting the Bible. Indeed, the influence of religion on morality is now so inconspicuous that it is possible to know a person fairly well for many years, and be familiar with his views on a variety of moral problems, without being able to tell whether he is a Christian or not, or if so to which sect of Christianity he subscribes. Some sects have characteristic rules: good Catholics do not use contraceptives, good Quakers do not serve in the armed forces, and there are quite a lot of things that Christadelphians and Plymouth Brethren may not do. But in general there is nothing in the way of moral principle that will clearly distinguish an Anglican or Methodist from an atheist or agnostic.

How has this decline of religious influence affected our moral standards? There still are religious people who argue as though there can be no moral standards at all without religious belief, so that a failure of religious belief must lead to a failure of moral conviction of every kind. This is perhaps true of some individuals, who have been brought up in the belief that morality is entirely dependent on religion, and the love and fear of God are the only adequate reasons for being good, and so tend to abandon their moral convictions when they abandon their belief in God. But clearly it is not true in general: there are plenty of earnest and upright atheists and agnostics. A man without religious faith lacks one important incentive to moral conduct, but not the only incentive.

Nevertheless, our system of moral instruction has for centuries been linked with Christianity. The Christian churches have been the main teachers and upholders of moral principles, the main agencies concerned to stimulate moral earnestness and devotion, urging people to seek first the kingdom of God and His righteousness, to put the moral law first in their lives rather than prosperity, comfort, reputation or fashion. As the influence of the churches wanes, it is not replaced by any other agency of comparable enthusiasm and effectiveness in arousing moral aspiration. The totalitarian countries have their substitutes in the form of political organizations; we have none. Thus it is to be expected that a falling-off in religious practice will be accompanied by a falling-off in moral devotion, by an increasing inclination to treat moral concerns as secondary rather than primary in the conduct of life; and this was one feature which we found in the new outlook. It is not that when a man loses the habit of church-going he also loses his moral convictions; it is that he no longer has anyone to remind him of them.

The content of the morality taught by the Christian churches has varied a great deal from one place and time to another. But there are certain constant features of Christian moral teaching to which the newer morality of our time is opposed. Christians have always held that the only permissible kind of sexual intercourse is that between husband and wife. And they have always held that wrongdoing proceeds from wickedness or sin, and that it deserves punishment as a just retribution; without this retributive principle the doctrine of Heaven and Hell and the doctrine of Atonement make no sense. Further, whatever the differences in detail amongst the churches, it is inevitable that a revealed religion should hold to the doctrine of eternal and immutable divine moral laws, and should refuse to accept human happiness or convenience as an adequate criterion of right and wrong. Here also contemporary morality diverges from the religious standpoint.

In place of the religious world-picture, that of the natural sciences is becoming increasingly prevalent. Of course, there is no outright incompatibility between a religious and a scientific point of view. It is both logically and psychologically possible to combine belief in almost any scientific theory with almost any kind of religious faith. Similarly, science neither requires nor refutes any particular moral principles. Science informs us of the way things are; and such information cannot possibly settle for us how we are to judge that things ought to be. It reveals to us the bounds of the possible; within these bounds we are always at liberty to prefer one possibility to another. If something is discovered by scientists to be inevitable, then it is not a matter for moral judgement; we are bound to put up with it, but we are not bound to approve of it. Thus there can be no such thing as a scientific morality, or even a scientifically based morality. Scientific research can perhaps tell us how to prevent the conception of unwanted babies, or how to improve the genetic constitution of those who are born. But whether we are to prefer a larger population or a higher standard of living, whether it is right to infringe the freedom to propagate in order to improve the quality of the race, these are questions to which scientific research, by virtue of its terms of reference, can give no answer.

Nevertheless, there is an influence exerted by scientific modes of thinking upon our moral standards. For the person accustomed to think scientifically is accustomed to operate with a certain set of ideas; and when he comes to think about non-scientific problems, in particular about ethical problems, he brings with him his accustomed set of ideas and tends to use them in this different field of thought. Now the scientific study of man is a part of biology. In biology, a man is regarded as a living organism, engaged in the endeavour to survive. The biological interpretation of human life is in terms of the attempt of the organism to adapt its environment to serve its own need for survival, and to adapt itself to the conditions imposed upon it by the environment, including the social environment in which the human organism grows up. Moral values as such do not fit very easily into this kind of interpretation. But there is a place in it for values of another kind, namely the value of success in surviving and the disvalue of failure to survive, the value of health and efficiency and the disvalue of disease and weakness. So a biologist attacking a social or moral problem thinks of it most readily as a problem of finding healthy adjustments to dangerous situations, of devising techniques for ensuring survival at a high level of efficiency. The useful as against the harmful, the healthy as against the diseased, the normal as against the abnormal, these are the contrasted conditions which a scientist can recognize; right and wrong in any other sense are outside his scientific purview. Such a point of view favours the idea of variable moral standards, which men can alter so as to adapt them to changes in the conditions under which they live. It favours the idea that there are basic human needs to be satisfied, and that any frustration of these needs is bad. It favours regarding human delinquency impersonally and dispassionately, as inefficient maladjustments resulting from the operation of universal laws of behaviour, rather than as the arbitrary wickedness of free and responsible persons, to be visited with retribution. In these ways the increasing prevalence of scientific modes of thought harmonizes with the ethical trend we have been tracing.

# V · The Psychiatrists

Amongst men of science, it is the students of human nature – the psychologists and sociologists – whose findings are most directly relevant to moral problems. We might therefore expect to find that the strongest influence of scientific ways of thinking upon moral standards is that of psychological science. There seems to be plenty of evidence that this is so. Professional psychologists give advice to troubled individuals on the proper way of conducting their lives, to parents and school-teachers on the best way of handling misbehaving children, to magistrates on the proper treatment of misbehaving adults (though we are yet far from the American situation in which the psychiatrist takes the place of the father confessor, and consulting him when in trouble becomes part of ordinary routine). And the advice is received with respect based on the scientific standing of the psychologist, a respect which the present-day priest can less easily command. This influence belongs principally to a particular group of psychologists, those who are mainly concerned with mental disease. It is the medical psychologists whose work most closely and obviously concerns moral issues; it is they who speak most loudly and distinctly on these issues; it is their theories which have most caught the public attention and suggested to the layman new and unfamiliar ways of thinking about himself. Freud is outstanding amongst psychologists as an intellectual influence on this generation.

The concern of the psychiatrist is with mental health. In so far as people are familiar with and responsive to the psychologist's approach to moral problems, they tend also to be preoccupied with health rather than with rectitude. The question they ask themselves in their private musings is not "Am I saved?" or "Am I good?", but "Am I a mature personality or a neurotic?" (The fear of being queer can, of course, be just as acute as the fear of being wicked, or even of being damned.) If they want to insult their neighbours, they call them, not cads or bounders, but "immature" or "insecure". This preoccupation goes along with a similar concern for physical health which has accompanied the general advance of medical knowledge.

One might suppose that to put the idea of mental health in place of the idea of virtue would be to substitute a relatively determinate, objective standard for one relatively subjective, disputable and uncertain. Ideas of what is right and wrong can vary widely, and some of them have been very strange indeed. But if we concentrate our attention on making people psychologically healthy, may we not hope to avoid much of the controversy and extravagance involved in the pursuit of subjective moral standards?

The matter is however more complicated than this. The standard of *physical* health is objective, in that there are straightforward ways of distinguishing between the ill and the well which are quite independent of our moral preferences, and on which everyone can agree. The healthy man can do a day's work, walk upstairs without puffing, eat a square meal without getting indigestion, and so forth. But there is no such straightforward test of what constitutes psychological well-being. There are of course extreme cases where there can be no disagreement. Some people cannot learn to talk intelligibly or do up their shoe-laces; other people imagine that they are members of the royal family, or are so lost in their fantasies that they cannot rouse themselves to eat their dinners. But apart from these obvious cases, what constitutes mental health, balance, adjustment, integration, maturity, is a matter on which there may well be much dispute. In the determination of this question we cannot avoid some value-judgements. If a man is eccentric, moody, difficult to get on with, unable to keep regular hours, but at the same time a great success in his chosen profession, how much does his professional competence count against the unfavourable judgement we might otherwise pass on his personality? Must he be urged to remedy his abnormalities of behaviour at the risk of drying up the springs of his inspiration? Is the healthy and mature personality to be distinguished by his capacity to satisfy himself and his own dominant interests (Hitler, for example, was conspicuously successful on this score), or must he also be able to satisfy the demands other people make on him? (This is not an issue that arises in the case of physical health.) One might say, of course, that a man cannot satisfy himself without to some extent satisfying other people's demands. But this is true only with large reservations; one wonders, for example, whether there is adequate evidence for the proposition, quite often asserted by psychiatrists, that no one can be happy without love.

If however we grant that one test of mental health must be the capacity to satisfy the social requirements of the community in which one lives, these requirements, of course, vary very widely from one community to another. Plenty of people who might at an earlier period of history have been regarded either as holy or as witches are now classified as lunatics. Plenty of behaviour-patterns which would have been accepted, and even admired, in the society of the Vikings are now treated as pathological. Thus the moral standards of the community enter into the criteria distinguishing mental health from mental disease. This is particularly plain in the concept of the psychopath, whose deficiencies are defined entirely in moral terms. And the same individual, with the same dispositions, may well be counted healthy in one community and not in another. Thus, given that an individual is unable to accommodate himself to the demands of his society or to live contentedly under the conditions it imposes, one has the choice of saying either that there is something wrong with him or that there is something wrong with the social conditions. This choice cannot be made without reference to moral standards. To classify a person as neurotic because he fails to fit in with the conditions under which he has to live is to give one's approval to those conditions as being of a kind which a man may be reasonably expected to tolerate. To classify homosexuality as an illness or perversion which one may hope to "cure" is to make a moral rather than a medical judgement; for it is not at all clear that homosexuality prevents a person from achieving happiness in life, if one discounts the handicaps imposed on him by a society such as ours, which (unlike some others) regards homosexuality as disgraceful. There is, then, no hope of getting from psychology an interpretation of the good life which shall be free from moral preconceptions. In judging this man to be healthy and that man diseased, the psychologist is bound to make some use of his own standards of good and evil, and some reference to those of his society.

Thus the influence of psychological theory on moral standards is not an altogether independent influence: its direction depends in part on the moral standpoint of the psychologists themselves. When one examines what the psychiatrists have written, and especially what they have written for the perusal of the general public, one gets the impression of a system of moral values whose keywords are "integration", "balance", "inner security", "adjustment", "harmony". The main emphasis in the concept of mental health is on the removal of conflict: in the first place, conflict in the individual's mind, so that he is not hampered by incompatible desires, uncertainties of purpose, doubt or distrust or dislike of himself, but becomes satisfied with himself and confident of what he wants to do. In the second place, there is the removal of conflict with the environment, by making him more contented, more able and willing to co-operate with other people, less inclined to long for what he has not got. Both these are of course excellent ideals. But the stressing of them perhaps begs some ethical questions which ought not to be begged.

The emphasis on inner harmony favours the placid, the cautious, the superficial, the limited approach to life as against the indulgence of passionate, perilous, absorbing enthusiasms. For if you allow yourself to be profoundly stirred by something, or deeply committed to it, you lay yourself open to the risk of equally profound frustration, and of inner conflict with your responses to other things that stir you. Great achievement is often associated with unbalance and lopsidedness of the personality, with the frustrating and renouncing of many natural interests outside the main field of endeavour, with a persistent restlessness and turbulence of soul. The safest way of avoiding conflict is not to let anything move you very strongly. We may envy the best-integrated personalities, but the people we most *admire* are more likely to show considerable signs of strain, of having had hard struggles with themselves to live the kind of lives they were resolved to lead, of having exercised some coercion on a reluctant personality to make it do what was required of it. Sometimes integration can be achieved only on a level which leaves one's finest powers unused; and where this is so, it may be worth while unbalancing and frustrating oneself in order to reach the most sublime experiences of which one is capable.

As to the second element in the ideal, integration with one's fellows, or "adjustment", a great stress on the need for the individual to adjust himself to his environment may also beg fundamental questions. Surely, there are some environments which one ought not to adjust to, but to struggle against? To preach "adjustment" is often to assume that, in the conflicts between the individual and his environment, it is the individual rather than the environment that is in the wrong, it is he who should be altered to conform to the environment rather than the other way about. The business of the army psychiatrist is to turn maladjusted soldiers into satisfactory soldiers, taking the existence, aims and organization of the army for granted. The business of the personnel manager in industry is to turn maladjusted and discontented workers into more contented and more efficient workers, taking for granted the existence, the purposes and the structure of the industry. Of course, the psychiatrist's business is to enable men to live tolerable lives in society as it is, and not to reform society so that it will be easier for men to live tolerable lives in it. (He will, all the same, have some responsibility to make known his findings about the sort of social institutions which are most productive of mental strain.) In consequence, there is a definite likelihood that one will find the psychiatrist lined up alongside the magistrate, the schoolmaster and the priest as a defender of the established order against criticism and discontent. This tendency is reinforced by the need to judge mental health by a concept of the "normal", and to assess the degree of a person's derangement by the extent to which he diverges from the normal. It is then very hard to avoid assuming that the average level of pugnacity, extraversion, sexuality, acquisitiveness, industry or amenability to discipline to be found in existing society is the right and proper level, and everybody who diverges from it must have something wrong with him. There are dangers in this. For not only is the conventional personality certain to be unsuitable as a model for many individuals who are temperamentally ill-fitted to become normally aggressive or compliant, normally gregarious or self-sufficient, normally sexy, without strain; but also the conventions themselves may be imperfect and stand in need of criticism and reform.

In considering the detailed connections between the increased influence of psychiatric modes of thought and recent changes in moral outlook, there is first one general point to be made. The best-known psychological theories of the twentieth century, by contrast with earlier psychologies, have laid great emphasis on the compulsive, neurotic character of much that formerly passed for conscientious behaviour. There have been various accounts, more or less lucid, more or less plausible, of the way in which the moral standards of a child's parents are "introjected" or "internalized"; but there has been quite a wide measure of agreement that some such process must take place. The formation of conscience is said to be a response to parental suggestion which is somehow motivated by the feelings attaching a child to his parents. Thereby conscience has been exhibited as basically an emotional response, lacking in rationality, lacking in any kind of authority or justification beyond that of the personal preferences of the parents.

This tracing of conscience to its infantile roots has had the effect of discrediting it; how could one take seriously a mode of thinking and feeling so little affected by understanding, so easily capable of absurdity, so hard to distinguish from neurosis?[1] For while no reputable psychologist wished to say that all conscientiousness is foolish, that there is no difference between being neurotic and trying to be good, few of them gave very clear indications of the difference between reasonable and unreasonable forms of conscientiousness, and many dwelt with gusto on the absurdities of which the conscience was capable, and the disastrous effects on many personalities of trying to live up to an exalted ideal. The effort to be moral often appears in psychiatric writing as the main cause, even the sole cause, of mental unbalance. Much has been written about the dangerous folly of building up an ideal picture of oneself and refusing to recognize the distance between this ideal picture and one's real character, about the devastating conditions of distress and uselessness which can result from feelings of guilt in failing to live up to exacting moral standards.

In so far as this teaching about the nature and origin of conscience is taken in earnest, the more serious and responsible people are set to wondering whether their own moral convictions are not after all neurotic, babyish and absurd. Moral earnestness itself comes under suspicion of being immature, as well as old-fashioned. The man who protests with vehemence against injustice, dishonesty or laziness can be dismissed with a snigger as trying to compensate for his own insecurity. The

[1] "Psycho-analysis had in fact done something to undermine conventional morality; it had revealed a certain clumsiness and crudity in the operations of man's powers of moral control, and shown with a clarity that had never before been attained that conscience was a factor in the mind that was capable of doing harm as well as good. . . . Neurosis, according to psycho-analytic findings, was due to conflict between repressed desires and a repressing (moral) force. . . . Freud had unmasked the pretensions of conscience as the perfect guide, exposed the primitive crudity of the repressing forces" (J. C. Flugel, *Man, Morals and Society*, pp. 31–33).

morally indifferent can protect themselves with a picture of the really grown-up person as one without conscientious scruples, who does whatever is most convenient to himself and accepts his own vices with equanimity. The general effect of this debunking of the conscience has been to shake the confidence of morally serious men in their own positions, to render all moral earnestness suspect and a little ridiculous. Thus the psychological theorists have substantially contributed to the tendency to take moral considerations less seriously, to edge the conscience on to the periphery of life.

In the Christian tradition, and also in a strong romantic strain within humanism, great value has been placed on conscientiousness as such, on having one's heart in the right place, on the mere endeavour to be virtuous, however unreflective and uninstructed. Sincerity and good intentions, it has often been assumed, are enough in themselves to constitute virtue, and to ensure that what one does will be morally valuable. The psychologists have undermined this simple faith. They have exposed the primitive mental processes by which conscience is formed. They have drawn attention to the amount of harm that can be done by sincere and well-intentioned people, for instance in the training of their children. But above all, they have revealed unsuspected possibilities of self-deception which may prevent men from discovering what their real intentions are. If our fundamental motives are after all largely unconscious, then the conscious assurance of sincerity and good intentions is insufficient to show that the intentions really are good. Fear, hatred, self-assertion may simulate moral principle in a masquerade impenetrable to the agent himself. The attitude which emerges from this is closer to Oriental moral philosophies than to any previously prevalent in Europe: the way to perfection does not pass through moral effort, but through self-examination and self-knowledge, an examination unlikely to succeed unless it is conducted under the guidance of an expert or guru who understands one better than one understands oneself.

As to the more detailed changes in moral attitude which we originally noted – the lower value attached to sexual restraint and sexual reticence, the increased tendency to give children what they fancy rather than what their parents think they ought to have, the movement towards "treating" instead of punishing criminals, the greater permissiveness of present-day morality and the general rejection of responsibility – when one considers the sort of argument by which these changes are defended, it seems plausible to give much of the credit or discredit for the changes themselves to the teachings of the psychologists. Has it not been learned from psychological investigation that sexual restraint is dangerous, that a strict upbringing is likely to lead to mental instability, that crime is often the consequence of deep psychological causes which can be modified by psychiatry but not by imprisonment, and is not the change in current attitudes the consequence of learning from the psychologists truths about human nature of which previous generations were unaware?

This interpretation of the facts is plausible at first sight; nevertheless we do not think there is much truth in it. There are some scientific theories, such as the Darwinian doctrine of evolution by natural selection, which have come to be accepted by the general thinking public because they have first been accepted by the consensus of scientific opinion based on plentiful and convincing evidence. But no general theory of human nature which has much relevance to morals stands in this position. Not many principles in psychology can be regarded as scientifically proved; and of those that can, few have any evident connection with moral principles. The sort of psychological theory which has chiefly influenced moral ideas is the sort which has the smallest claim to any scientific authority. Psychiatrists belong to a number of different schools of thought, roundly and sometimes violently contradicting one another's basic principles, so that none of them can speak with the authority of established scientific doctrine. It is not by producing evidence adequate to convince the general opinion of psychologists that Freud, for instance, has gained his influence over contemporary thinking; indeed, the Freudian movement has sometimes borne more of the marks of an evangelist crusade than of a scientific investigation. One must therefore look for other reasons for the popularity of such ideas than the strength of the arguments behind them.

Presumably these ideas fitted in with a movement of thought and sentiment which was already taking place; they suggested to people what they were already disposed to believe. Where they did not, comparatively little notice was taken of them. There is as much in psycho-analytic theory about the ill-effects of spoiling children as about the ill-effects of bullying them. If modern parents and their advisers have taken much notice of the evils of severity and little notice of those of indulgence, it is probably because they were thereby encouraged in a course they already wished to pursue. Perhaps, having themselves lost confidence in the moral standards which their parents imposed on *them*, they are ready to make the most of any reasons the psychologists can provide for not imposing these standards on their own children. Thus the claim that psychological theory has been a strong independent influence on changes in values is subject to large reservations. Since so much in the relevant branches of psychology is matter of opinion rather than proved fact, and since psychologists themselves are influenced by movements of thought outside their own subject, we must regard psychological theory as *resulting* from changes in moral outlook as well as provoking them.

What, in fact, has psychological investigation established that is relevant to the matters we are discussing? As to sexual morality, there is good evidence that great damage to mental health can be caused by the repression of sexual desire, using "repression" in its technical sense, in which it involves not merely depriving sexual desire of its natural outlet, but also refusing to acknowledge its existence or its strength in oneself. There is good evidence that a great deal of neurotic disturbance has been caused by sexual desires whose existence their possessors have refused to face, either because they were adulterous, incestuous or otherwise reprehensible, or because the individuals thought it shameful to admit to having sexual appetites at all. Repression of sexual desire in this sense can produce distortions of the personality, as can the repression of many other kinds of desire. Thus there exists ample evidence in favour of one aspect of the change in our sexual morality, the change towards open acknowledgement of sexual appetites and interests and open discussion of sexual issues. But there is no reliable evidence to show that one cannot live tolerably happily without sexual gratification. The idea of successfully "sublimating" sexual desires, that is, taking other gratifications as replacements for the sexual, is Freud's own. Nor is there any convincing evidence to show that a looser sexual morality is more conducive to human happiness than a stricter one.

As to the upbringing of children, there are a few matters on which the psychological investigators seem to be pretty well agreed. It is essential for the adequate development of a child's personality, of his capacity to cope with life's problems and find happiness for himself, that in infancy he should have confidence that he is loved by somebody who takes care of him – usually and preferably his mother. The lack of such love or, still worse, the loss of it when it has been enjoyed, represents a risk, and very likely the most serious risk, of deforming the child's character. Given the fundamental confidence of being constantly loved, a child can survive a good deal of frustration and many unpleasant experiences without psychological disaster. It is also agreed that the experience of being intensely frightened can have lasting ill effects on a child's nerves, more severe than frightening experiences in adult life. Thus one may read in the psychological treatises and case histories a clear condemnation of the cruel parent, of the regular use of terror as a means of discipline, of the principle of breaking a child's will in order to enforce obedience. If the parental bully is a rarer figure in contemporary England than in the past, as we believe he or she is, then the psychologists can take some of the credit for this. There is an equally clear condemnation of the neglectful and indifferent parent.

But affection is not inconsistent with discipline. There is no agreed professional opinion and no body of convincing evidence to show that comparatively permissive methods of bringing up children are either more efficient or less efficient than comparatively strict methods in producing capable, self-controlled, cheerful young people. It looks as though neither severity in itself nor laxity in itself is as dangerous as a wayward vacillation between the two, which prevents a child from achieving an adjustment to his situation because he never knows what he has to adjust to. Nevertheless it seems that parents who take notice of the psychologists' findings, who are aware of the importance of giving their children a firm consciousness of being loved, will naturally lean to the side of indulgence, since letting the child have his own way may well seem the most reliable proof of affection.

But perhaps the most important effect of publicizing modern psychological theories is not connected with any specific advice they give. It arises from bringing into prominence the great importance of early experience in the formation of character, and the many ways in which a person's chances of happiness can be marred by faulty treatment in infancy. On the whole our grandparents regarded bringing up children as an arduous and exacting task, requiring much labour and patience, but not as a technically difficult task, requiring expert knowledge or special skill – it was like plain cooking, the sort of thing which any woman might be expected to master by the exercise of a little common sense. Now that so much has been heard of complexes, frustrations, inhibitions, repressions and the rest, the modern parent cannot easily take this confident line. She is aware that bringing up children is a difficult art, that there are a great many ways in which even an affectionate and conscientious parent can unwittingly set up harmful attitudes in a child. This makes the well-informed modern parents more thoughtful, more inclined to take allegedly expert advice, readier to ponder the effects of their methods of training on their children's characters, less apt to react to childish behaviour (especially childish misbehaviour) in the passion of the moment. It also makes them more nervous and anxious in face of their responsibilities as trainers, less confident and assured in giving their children instructions. Perhaps this hesitancy itself lessens the disciplinary hold they have over the children. Inevitably, the psychologists' preoccupations are with the various things that can go wrong with the training of children. It might help a little if they reminded parents more often of the toughness and resilience of ordinary human nature, of the large numbers of turbulent and insubordinate children, nervous and timid children, sullen and listless children, who manage nevertheless to grow up into competent and cheerful adults. Nature no more demands perfect child-rearing from parents than perfect behaviour from children. Psychologists have often justly reproached the preachers of past generations for filling people with the terror of damnation. But there are plenty of psychological writings which leave their more suggestible readers filled with a conviction of inescapable psychological deformity.

The question of criminal responsibility is rather different. For while one cannot say that psychologists as a body have recommended any specific changes in sexual morality or standards of child discipline, there has been a good deal of pressure from those psychologists who have been especially concerned with criminal behaviour towards modifying the general attitude to crime and criminals. The modification they have advocated, not without success, is the partial replacement of the guilt-punishment attitude to criminals by the illness-treatment attitude, the transference of some types of criminals from the category of wilful morally responsible wrongdoers, to be dealt with by punishment, to the category of mentally deranged persons to be dealt with by psychiatric treatment. (There is, of course, an element of corporate self-interest in this pressure, since such a change enhances the importance of psychiatrists.) On what grounds can such a transference be justified?

The question is sometimes discussed on the assumption that there are two mutually exclusive categories of offenders against the law, those who are sane and normal and therefore blameworthy, and those who are insane or abnormal and therefore blameless; that to place an individual in one category is thereby to exclude him from the other; and that every offender must belong squarely inside one of the two categories. This assumption is surely mistaken. The only reasonably sharp distinction that can be drawn in this matter is the distinction of the M'Naughten rules between those who do and those who do not understand what they are doing and whether it is wrong (i.e. forbidden by law). All other distinctions between sanity and insanity, mental health and disease, normality and abnormality, are distinctions of degree, in which the entirely balanced, rational, self-controlled individual (if such individuals exist) passes into the raving lunatic by a series of small steps. Everybody is a bit queer in some ways; everybody has a certain measure of understanding and self-control.

When a crime is committed, it is always possible to point to something in the personality of the criminal which differentiates him from normal people, who do not commit crimes. He may be subject to uncommonly strong bursts of temper, he may be seeking compensation for the affection his mother never gave him, he may have a very low I.Q., suffer from a drug addiction or a sexual perversion. . . . Since the normal person is law-abiding (except when driving a car), it is easy enough to make criminal behaviour a symptom of abnormality, and "All criminals are abnormal" true by definition. Misbehaviour always has causes, and the causes are necessarily to be found in some circumstances of character or situation which do not affect the well-behaved. It is highly desirable to discover as much as we can of the nature of these causes and the means of prevention and cure. But to discover the causes of misbehaviour, and even to discover them in mental dispositions of the kind that psychiatrists can modify, is not to prove this misbehaviour irresponsible and exempt from blame and punishment. There is no inconsistency in saying of an offender "This man is mentally diseased, and requires treatment" and also saying of him "This man is guilty, and deserves punishment". A man is bad if he wilfully and deliberately does evil; and he may be reasonably and justly punished if he has wilfully done evil, and if there is ground for expecting that the punishment will produce an improvement in his behaviour. And these things, though they cannot be true of a man who is insane in the sense of the M'Naughten rules, may well be true of an offender of marked mental abnormality. To account for a piece of human behaviour is not necessarily to excuse it.

It may, indeed, happen that as one studies and comes to understand the frame of mind of those who do wrong, as one comes to see anti-social behaviour as the natural, perhaps the inevitable outcome of the forces of heredity and environment, as one says to oneself "There, but for the grace of God (or the shuffling of the chromosomes) go I", so resentment against vice tends to evaporate, and even be replaced by sympathy for the vicious. ("*Tout comprendre, c'est tout pardonner*".) But, as the feeling of resentment is an inadequate reason for inflicting punishment, so its absence is an inadequate reason for remitting it. Whether a man should be held morally responsible for his offences and liable to punishment for them is not to be determined by the resentment or sympathy felt towards him by other people. Nor is it to be determined by the place he occupies on the scale between the perfectly sane and normal and the perfectly insane or queer; for how could we possibly decide at what point on this scale the line was to be drawn?

Of course, if it could be shown that the commission of an offence was due to an impulse which was irresistible, in the sense that the offender could not prevent himself from so acting however hard he tried, then this offence could not be accounted morally responsible, for the notion of moral responsibility applies only to actions which are within the control of choice. Nor could such an action reasonably be punished, since punishment does not induce a man to control the uncontrollable. But it is extremely difficult to show that any given impulse on any given occasion *was* irresistible. Even if we take a man's word for it that he tried to resist the impulse, how can we know – how can he himself know – that he tried as hard as he could? It may be doubted whether the impulse to commit a crime is ever absolutely irresistible in the way that sneezing can be – even kleptomaniacs somehow manage not to steal things when somebody else is watching them. One can scarcely do more towards proving the irresistibility of an impulse than to show that it is often not resisted; and it would be paradoxical if an offender could cite his previous bad conduct as exempting him from responsibility for his actions!

The right ground for drawing the distinction between those offenders who are properly to be blamed and punished and those who are not seems to us to be this. The purpose of punishment and censure is to influence behaviour. If it should turn out that there is a class of offenders on whom punishment and censure have no appreciable effect, the reason for condemning and punishing these offenders disappears. If a person is so constituted mentally that he does not respond to moral exhortation it is no use exhorting him. If he is so constituted that he does not respond to threats of punishment, or even to punishment itself, to punish him is futile vindictiveness. It is for this reason that the man who does not understand what he does is not morally responsible; for he cannot respond either to appeals or to threats unless he knows what he is doing. It is for this reason also that irresistible impulse, if it could be proved, would be a valid excuse. But this line of reasoning does not lead to a classification of offenders into the sane or normal on the one hand, and the insane or abnormal on the other. It leads to a distinction between the corrigible and the incorrigible. Clearly this is a distinction of degree, and not a hard-and-fast line. Clearly, also, to classify an offender as incorrigible is not to say that there is no wickedness in him; it is not the same as clearing or absolving him.

In so far as he is not responsive to moral and legal sanctions, he is not, at least in respect of this type of offence, a responsible person and a member of the moral community. But he is still a nuisance, and some other way of dealing with him must be found. This alternative way may be gentler than punishment; it may not. Some kinds of "curative treatment" are very disagreeable, and if offered a choice between a long spell in prison and a long spell in a mental hospital one might well hesitate to make up one's mind. The choice we make between liquidation, punishment, preventive detention and psychiatric treatment must depend on our judgement of the likely efficacy of the various alternatives. Thus the boundary we draw between those who are regarded as morally responsible and dealt with by a combination of exhortation and punishment, and those who are regarded as mentally ill and dealt with by psychiatric methods, may well shift as the skill of psychiatrists improves. We have argued that there is no theoretical inconsistency between regarding an offender as blameworthy and regarding him as psychologically abnormal. The inconsistency is practical; since it is difficult to combine punishment with treatment, we usually have to come down on one side or the other. As psychologists become more expert at remedying psychological disorders, it is reasonable to shift more offenders from the moral to the medical category. There was a time when madmen were flogged to drive the devil out of them, and this method of treatment seems to have been not wholly ineffective. Now that we know more about insanity, we treat our mental cases differently; though possibly shock therapy is not so different from flogging in its mode of operation as we would like to think.

Thus to make a case for treating a given class of offenders as sick persons to be treated rather than as guilty persons to be punished, it is not enough to show that their misbehaviour is the result of some abnormality of mind. It must also be shown that medical treatment is likely to be as effective as the usual legal penalties in preventing a recurrence of the offences in question. And here one cannot determine the issue entirely by considering the effect of treatment or punishment on the individual offender alone. One must also take into account the effects on other potential offenders. To argue "This boy has a thing about breaking windows, and will go on breaking windows even if I thrash him for it; therefore I must let him off the thrashing" would be sound reasoning if one had only this boy to consider. But if a headmaster in charge of a schoolful of boys acts on this reasoning, he may well find that he has an epidemic of window-breaking on his hands. There are occasions on which it is right to punish an offender, knowing pretty well that punishment will not improve his behaviour, but hoping that it will improve the behaviour of others, who will take warning from his fate, or who will regard it as an injustice if he is excused.

We have seen that the trend towards a more permissive morality has been reinforced by the influence of the medical psychologists, though they did not initiate it. They have not however been able to show with certainty that a permissive way of life is more favourable to human happiness than old-fashioned strictness. On this question, we need far more information than we have at present. What the psychiatrists have done by their probing into the origins of conscience is to shake our confidence in our moral sentiments and moral traditions. So, while we have become more candid and more open-minded, we have also become much more diffident in our attempts to discipline our children, our criminals and our own sexual impulses.

# VI · The Publicity Men

Besides the psychologists, there is another group of people whose influence on moral ideas seems to be increasing. These are the publicity men. In the rapidly changing circumstances of twentieth-century life, custom and tradition have a comparatively weak influence on our ways of thinking. And those groups of people who have enjoyed a prestige based on their knowledge of traditional skills, from peers of the realm to elderly craftsmen and grandmothers, have lost much of their authority. When tradition loses its force, fashion takes over. When men cease to respect their elders or the classes above them in the social scale, they imitate the majority of their fellows. When they can no longer get security and confidence from the feeling that they are in the right, they get a second-best kind of security from the feeling that they are at least in the swim, doing what everybody else is doing, keeping up with the Joneses. Hence the spread of "other-directedness", and the cult of group at the expense of individual experience. It therefore becomes of great importance, in a society dominated by fashion rather than tradition, to find out who sets the fashion.

Now setting the fashion is a craft and a business, the craft and business of those who operate the organs of mass publicity. Their prominence in modern society is the result of the availability of the so-called mass media, the newspapers and magazines, radio and television programmes, which are read or listened to by millions of people at once. These make it possible for a man or a group of men, skilled at putting ideas into people's heads, to put the same idea at once into the heads of vast numbers, a thing not possible in earlier times.

The mass media differ in another way from older means of persuasion such as personal conversation, preaching, or books, when books were few. Ideas put over in these old-fashioned ways were generally taken in a few at a time, digested slowly, pondered and argued over. Ideas put over by the mass media are presented in a quite different context. Broadcasting programmes succeed one another all day. Newspapers and magazines are not read, but skimmed or glanced at over the breakfast table, in the bus or train, at the hairdresser's; what they say is rarely given much attention, pondered or debated. This is still more obviously true of the advertisements on the hoardings which one sees out of the corner of one's eye in passing. Hence the techniques which are most effective in these contexts are apt to differ from those most effective in older forms of persuasion. Reading and hearing so much more than our grandparents, we pay proportionately less attention to what we do read. Those old gentlemen who had read the Bible right through half a dozen times read little else; but they knew what was in the Bible. Our contemporaries read the daily paper every morning, and a week later remember nothing that was in it.

Consequently, the skill of using the mass media to influence opinion is the skill of bringing it about that an idea that is subject only to a momentary attention is nevertheless firmly lodged in the mind of the hearer or reader. The sensationalist approach, the extravagant language, the endless repetition, the jingles, the wisecracks, are all devices for securing this end. More recently, psychological research has suggested another such device – the associating of the desired idea with some other idea which already has stability and insistence because it carries strong emotion or longing. The publicity men are the masters of these techniques, the techniques of hooking us below the belt, of inducing us to do things without realizing why we do them, of leading us in a direction we have not deliberately chosen, but have been half-consciously coaxed or chivvied into.

This expertise they are prepared to sell to any buyer who makes a satisfactory offer, whether politician, soap manufacturer or evangelist. To that extent, publicity is neutral; anybody can use it who can afford to hire it: any doctrine can be propagated by its techniques. The ideas it will put across are those of its hirers, and not those of its operators: in Moscow the Bolshevik party, in New York the tycoons. It is clear that the mass media, in the hands of men of bad will, are capable of being very powerful instruments of tyranny and corruption, just as atom bombs are more powerful agents of destruction than muskets. In present-day Britain, the strongest influence in determining their character is the commercial gain of those who operate them, and of those who hire them in order to sell their goods.

In consequence the mass media subject all citizens to a powerful incitement to spend their money, and on the whole to spend it without discrimination. It is urged upon us that the secret of happy living is in the abundance and up-to-dateness of our possessions; that this or that article is indispensable to our well-being; that if we want to avoid being cut by our boy- and girl-friends we *must* use A's deodorant, that if we want to be free of drudgery and consequent ill-temper we *must* get B's up-to-the-minute fully-automatic washing-machine, that because we all drink C's beverage we're *happy* girls and boys. We are being taught to look for satisfaction in a breathless race to expand our stock of possessions. Our grandparents filled their children with anxiety about the state of their souls, or their conformity to the conventions. Our new mentors, the advertisers, are doing their damnedest to fill us with anxiety about the up-to-dateness of our household equipment.[1] If materialism means relying for our happiness on the acquisition of material goods, the message of the current mass media is materialistic.

Whoever directs it, mass-medium publicity is a moral influence in its own right, because the character of the technique itself favours some kinds of message as against others and promotes certain attitudes of mind in the practitioners and the consumers of this publicity. Because it operates by suggestion rather than by informing or arguing, it can far more easily put across ideas which are simple and superficial than those which are subtle, complex and profound; it can effectively impress a slogan on the public mind, but not a theory. Thriving on the habit of thinking in clichés and stereotypes, it necessarily encourages such thinking. Its best patrons, i.e. those most responsive to its suggestions, are the receptive, the uncritical, the half-awake minds. Its own interest is therefore to encourage such frames of mind.

There is another factor in the situation. Publicity is most effective when it appeals to the largest number of people. Those who sell newspapers or films are of course bent on attracting the largest possible public, for this is the way to make money. As regards newspapers, this drive towards large circulations is enormously strengthened by dependence on revenue

[1] "Our job is to make women unhappy with what they have. We must make them so unhappy that their husbands can find no happiness or peace in unnecessary saving." Quoted from a speech at an American advertising convention in *The American Invasion*, by Francis Williams.

from advertisements, since the value of an advertisement depends on the number of people it will reach. The conversational persuader, the door-to-door salesman or political go-between, will of course vary his approach according to the sort of person he is dealing with. But the mass persuader must say the same thing to all his listeners or readers. He will therefore say the thing that will make an impact on the largest possible number of those listeners or readers. That is to say, if he wishes to be successful he is bound to ignore everything distinctive or peculiar to any particular class or set of people, and to approach men on the basis of what is most universal, most ordinary, most commonplace. He dare not be above the head of the average member of his audience; to play safe he will prefer to be below it. He will endeavour to amuse and entertain, flatter and cajole, rather than to arouse an effort of thought which might be disturbing. He dare not cast doubt on any common value or prejudice; he dare not concern himself with matters of interest only to a minority. He must play upon and thereby reinforce those interests and points of view that are common to the largest possible number of potential customers for whatever kind of wares he has to purvey. Thus the picture of human nature he will present and strive to actualize in the audience will be as average and uniform as possible. The influence of mass publicity therefore will tend to encourage uniformity in outlook, tastes and standards; it will tend to reinforce whatever attitudes are already very common in the community and to discourage whatever attitudes are already very uncommon. The mass commercial advertisements seem to be directed at individuals with only two discernible passions, emulation and sex. The party political broadcasts seem to be directed at listeners who are politically ill-informed, lukewarm, conventional and selfish.

In so far as serious moral issues are touched on, the point of view adopted will be rather vaguely commonplace and conventional, and issues that cannot be handled without offending large groups of people will not be handled at all. But all challenging innovation, whether moral or aesthetic, offends many people; everybody with a serious faith to propound must tread hard on somebody's corns. Moral enthusiasts are likely to be reformers, that is, critics of established standards. Artistic movements with life in them are likely to be minority movements. The effect of the mass media will therefore be to shut out those ideas that have most life in them; or, if they are admitted, to dilute them with so much conventional soda-water that they cannot raise anyone's pulse. The classical examples of this are the numerous Hollywood adaptations of serious-minded books so as to turn them into replicas of innumerable other Hollywood productions. The more the mass media dominate our thinking, the greater the danger of moral and intellectual stagnation.

Of course, the commonplace standards may not be bad ones, as standards go. But even commonplace standards cannot be maintained without constant pressure from superior taste and superior morality. What keeps people up to scratch in their conduct is the aspiration after something rather better than the ordinary. The normal tendency of human nature, subject to all the temptations that come from the persistent conflict between the right and the convenient, is to become slacker and more indifferent. To counteract this tendency one needs fairly constant reminders of ideals higher than the everyday. Without some source of inspiration, people cease to aspire, they slack off. There are many indications that this is the tendency of contemporary society. The function of the weekly church service and the weekly sermon is to keep people reminded of standards higher than the average, to make demands on the worshipper rather more stringent than anyone expects him to fulfil. If the mass media are to take over the business of instructing and informing the public, they must provide it with a sufficiency of moral inspiration. And this they are unwilling to do, because it conflicts with their commercial purposes; it arouses sales resistance.

Another possible source of guidance in the formation of moral attitudes is serious fiction. At the present day this probably reaches a wider audience than ever before. Yet the impression we get from much reading of contemporary novels is that few of the novelists have any definite moral outlook to convey, either directly or by implication. Their work reflects the present uncertainties. Eager and expert at disparaging and debunking other men's standards, they fail to exhibit their own. By contrast with those of previous generations modern novels rarely present any characters as admirable, any standards of conduct as valid, any experiences and achievements as satisfying and worth while. (C. P. Snow is an exception to this tendency, and perhaps it is this rather than any outstanding literary ability that accounts for the popularity of his work.) It almost looks as though some novelists use fiction as a means of release from their own unpleasant experiences without regard to the effect on the reader. This expressionist approach parallels that already remarked in painting and music.

But since many people, especially young people, look to journalism or fiction for a lead in the present-day confusion of values, it is unfortunate that the lead they receive is so often towards moral nihilism.

# VII · The Philosophers

In this situation of changing values and changing sources of authority, where does philosophy stand? Is it not a proper task of moral philosophers to try to understand these changes, to interpret them to the public, and to assess the gains and losses associated with them? Is not the philosopher a worthy candidate for the role which the clergyman has lost and for which the publicity man possesses such inadequate qualifications?

This is indeed one of the functions of philosophy, according to the conception of philosophy generally held before the present century. But most professional philosophers in this country now hold the opposite opinion: that it is no proper part of philosophy either to understand the actual currents of moral opinion and their sources or to evaluate their merits and defects, and if any philosopher does this sort of thing he does it in an unprofessional capacity without benefit of his philosophical qualifications. To the outsider this may look like dodging a task which, though arduous and even hazardous, still needs to be done. But the modern philosophers have a powerful argument in favour of their view. It may be expressed thus.

Moral judgements, and in general all judgements of value, that is judgements to the effect that something is good or bad, right or wrong, ought or ought not to be done, is admirable, useful, beautiful, magnificent, deplorable, shady, progressive, reactionary, delightful, horrible and so forth, are of a different kind from judgements of science and history. In science and history, while there is necessarily much ignorance and disagreement, yet it is always possible in principle that the ignorance might be remedied and the disagreements resolved by the discovery of some piece of evidence which would conclusively settle the issue. We may not be sure of the truth, but we know what further information would make us sure, if only we could get it. But in the case of moral and other value judgements, it is possible for different people to disagree irreconcilably even when they are in possession of all the relevant information, so that no further evidence would bring them nearer agreeing. The reason for this is that to judge something good or bad, right or wrong, is not just to acknowledge the existence of certain facts, but also and principally to declare oneself for or against, to approve or disapprove, to avow a pro- or con-attitude. Such attitudes do not depend merely on the understanding of the facts, but also on the emotions and decisions of the persons making the judgement. Moral judgements, then, are at least in part expressions of feeling and are never properly speaking judgements of fact – for while there are scientific and historical facts, there are no moral facts. So moral judgements cannot be properly speaking either true or false; for truth and falsity belong to statements of fact, not to attitudes, emotions or decisions. Nor can moral judgements be either proved or disproved; for the words "prove" and "disprove" apply only to arguments that are logically conclusive to anybody who fully understands them, whereas moral judgement is determined not merely by the understanding, but by the passions and the will. To make a man accept a moral judgement one must make him feel or resolve something, and this is the task of the art of persuasion, not of the science of demonstration.

This philosophical view of morality is "subjective" in holding that the difference between right and wrong cannot be discovered in the external world, but is the consequence of emotions felt and decisions taken by each man for himself; and so different men can adopt different moral judgements without either of them being mistaken or accepting an untruth. Moral conflict, whether within a man or between one man and another, is a conflict of desires and wills, not a conflict of understanding.

If this subjectivist doctrine is correct, it follows that philosophy must be ethically neutral. For philosophy is an intellectual discipline, a pursuit of truth. Since in the moral field there are no truths to be discovered, philosophers must confine themselves to the logical analysis of moral judgement and moral reasoning. Any moral judgements they make will not be theoretical conclusions, but expressions of their own pro- and con-attitudes.

It should be noted that to say that moral judgements are matters of personal feeling and choice (not matters of knowledge), is *not* to say that any moral judgement is *as good as* any other. This would be itself a moral judgement, an expression of indifference as between different moralities. There is no reason why an ethical subjectivist should not have strong moral convictions – as, for instance, Lord Russell has. So, when subjectivism is attacked as a pernicious doctrine likely to lead to moral laxity, the subjectivist can reply that his theory is merely a logical analysis and has no ethical consequences; it is consistent with any kind of moral valuation, whether strict or lax.

Now as regards the *logical* consequences of subjectivism, this defence is certainly valid. But the effects of holding a theory are not limited to the logical consequences deducible from it. There are a number of ways in which subjectivism has an influence on moral attitudes, and its influence is in general favourable to the trends discussed in this book.

For firstly, when the logical positivists said that moral judgements were meaningless, however much they might explain away "meaningless" as a technical term, the emotive force of the expression, its disparaging overtones, still remained. If moral judgements cannot be true, cannot be proved, these are intellectual merits that they lack. They are moved out of the respectable company of scientific and historical hypotheses and classed along with exclamations like "Hurrah!" and "Blast!" and with the disreputable fakes of the "metaphysicians". Forming a moral judgement appears, not as an intellectually responsible and orderly procedure, but as an ebullition of feeling or a fiat of the will. To get a man to change his moral opinions one must employ the persuasive arts of the salesman, the mob orator or the confidence trickster, not the rigorous logic of the scientist. Since moral judgements are neither true nor capable of proof, the conclusion has been generally drawn that the making and advocacy of such judgements is no proper part of the intellectual discipline of philosophy. Moral philosophy, hitherto thought of as a critical examination of moral principles, must become a study of the meanings of the words in which those principles are expressed, and of the logical peculiarities of moral judgement and dispute. The issue is not merely what sense one is to give to the word "philosophy"; there is a good case for saying that these linguistic and logical inquiries cohere with the other traditional branches of philosophy to make one discipline in a way that the critical study of moral principles does not. But there is a more important issue: is the critical study of moral principles a serious and intellectually weighty subject of study, worthy of a place in an academic curriculum? The effect of the now prevalent re-definition of "philosophy" is to answer this question in the negative. For if it is not the business of philosophers, nor of social scientists – whose concern is, of course, with fact, not with valuation – there is no body of learned men concerned with it and no place for it in any university. (In fact many of the most noteworthy contemporary discussions of moral issues are carried on by specialists in literature, who are less inhibited by anxieties about the proper definition of their subject.) Such an attitude on the part of philosophers to the earnest examination of moral principles can hardly fail to encourage the general tendency to disparage moral earnestness, and to move morality from the centre towards the margin of human concerns.

Further, subjectivism is destructive of every kind of moral authority. If there is no moral truth to be known, nobody can know it. Nobody can be wiser than anyone else on matters of right and wrong, nobody can tell me with authority what I am to do in a moral dilemma in the way that a gardening expert can tell me how to grow chrysanthemums. Thus the result of adopting a subjectivist standpoint is that one feels entitled to ignore the moral opinions of other people, which after all only express their preferences. Therefore it must work against the power of custom, of the churches, or of older people to exercise restraint over the young.

Also, subjectivism accords better with laxer standards than with stricter ones. The model for the idea of objective morality is the law, a strict precise rule. But if morality is made to depend on preferences or pro-attitudes, these are not precise at all; they are various, vague, shifting and inconsistent. A morality based on authority can be strict and precise. But one based on pro-attitudes can hardly help accommodating itself to the variety and flexibility which these pro-attitudes possess. In the same way, subjectivism makes for fluid standards. If there are objective principles of right and wrong, then they are eternal, and do not change with changes in the tastes or opinions of men. But if moral judgements are no more than the expression of our preferences, they are bound to change as those preferences change along with age, diet, social relations, ways of earning a living and so forth. In other words, a subjectivist moralist sees no necessary impropriety in a man's fancying one style of morals today, another tomorrow, or a nation's changing its collective mind about the rules of behaviour that it wishes to follow. By contrast, an objectivist morality insists on consistency; I can change my mind about my moral principles only by convicting myself of some error. In all these ways the ethical subjectivism of the philosophers is in line with the trend towards a looser, less precise, more variable, less authoritative kind of morality such as we have found in contemporary society.

In this respect there is not a great deal of difference between the dominant trend in British philosophy and the existentialist type which has been flourishing in much of Europe. At first sight these two kinds of philosophy look wholly different; and indeed they are very different in their preoccupations and methods. But the ethical message they convey is very much the same. In morality there is no truth, no wisdom, nor can there be any authority. Fundamentally one's moral standpoint is and must be determined by one's own choice, made on one's own authority and responsibility. Sartre and Camus deny the possibility of moral reasoning, and stigmatize as self- deception the notion that rules of right and wrong can be discovered. Both philosophical movements insist that a man must decide on his own standards for himself, with no objective rule to guide him, and that no philosophical theory (or any other sort of theory) can make up his mind for him or demonstrate the superiority of one choice over another. Of both alike one can complain that the hungry sheep look up and are not fed; and both make the same reply, namely that the sheep are looking up in the wrong place – it is not the business of philosophy to provide moral guidance, since philosophy is concerned with the truth, and in morals there are no truths.

One consequence of the acceptance of a subjective interpretation of moral judgements is particularly worth attention. If there are indeed objective moral truths, then the way for a man to discover them is by the exercise of his intelligence, and the way for a community of men to discover them is by discussion and argument between many investigators. The proper way to settle ethical disputes will be by reasoning with those who disagree with you, and taking note of their arguments. The only moral opinions one is justified in holding are those based upon right reason. But if instead subjectivism is accepted, then the distinction between rational and irrational moral judgements disappears (except in so far as some judgements can be called irrational because they are internally inconsistent or based on mistakes of fact). Likewise the distinction between rational and irrational means of persuasion disappears. A moral conviction produced by intimidation, by drugs or brain surgery, by "brainwashing" or high-pressure advertising, is not for that reason any less rational, any less justifiable, than one produced as a result of a calm and careful review of a situation.

The traditional case for freedom of speech in matters of moral and political right and wrong, as we find it for instance in J. S. Mill, is based on the objectivist assumption that there are true and false opinions in morals which can be discovered and established by reasoning. On this assumption, we can maintain that any man having the use of reason is entitled to his own opinions about right and wrong unless they can be shown to be mistaken by rational argument. To try to alter them by any kind of psychological pressure is an injury to him, and a confession of intellectual inadequacy in those who apply the pressure. It is also an injury to society at large; for, the best hope of arriving at the truth being through full and free comparison of competing opinions, to prevent a man from expressing his own considered views is to deprive his fellow men of any enlightenment they might have derived from him.

But subjectivism destroys this case. For if subjectivism is true, the defence of freedom of speech on moral issues cannot be a defence of truth against error, but only a defence of one pro- or con-attitude against others. Galileo before the Inquisition will still have a case; for he puts forward an alleged truth which can and should be proved or disproved by rational consideration of the evidence. But Socrates before an Athenian jury, or the author of *Lady Chatterley's Lover* before an English one, will have no case, for he puts forward only his own likes and dislikes, which cannot be proved or disproved. His propaganda makes no contribution to knowledge, for moral convictions are not knowledge; and no truth can be lost by shutting his mouth. Nor can it be argued that the free ventilation of conflicting value-judgements is the best way to reach agreement. If there were accredited ways of proving such judgements, this might be so. But since there are none, the uncontrolled expression of conflicting differences is just as likely to lead to a breach of the peace as to a rapprochement.

Thus by abolishing the difference between rational and irrational persuasion, subjectivism removes one of the most important safeguards against the various kinds of coercion by which men may be made to change their valuations. And it can hardly fail to have some discouraging effect on any individual who wishes to stand up for his own dissenting valuations, since he can no longer think of himself as defending truth against error, but only as championing his own pro-attitudes against people who do not share them. Thus, in the struggle between individual responsibility and the convenience of the management, subjectivism seems the natural ally of the management. It does not seem reasonable to expect a man to forswear the truth for the general convenience; it does seem reasonable to expect him to adjust his pro- and con-attitudes to fit in better with other people's.

Before embarking on the critical appraisal of contemporary moral attitudes, it is advisable to consider just how far the subjectivist standpoint in ethics can be accepted. It seems to us that there *is* a large element of truth in subjectivism. It is true that a moral judgement is essentially the declaration of an attitude, a commitment or a decision. It is true that if a man cares nothing for the welfare of anybody but himself, or himself and his fellow-tribesmen, or if he has a horror of eating meat or getting his hair cut or being seen naked, he commits no intellectual error and there is no way of proving him to be mistaken – the concept of "mistake" does not apply here. But it does not follow that the difference between true and false, and the difference between reasonable and unreasonable, do not apply at all in the field of moral judgements. Admittedly, in so far as moral judgements merely express pro- and con-attitudes, no question of truth or falsity, reasonableness or unreasonableness, can arise; they are then just on the same level as tastes in food or company or any other sort of likes and dislikes.

But what distinguishes my mere likes and dislikes on the one hand from judgements of right and wrong on the other is my readiness to offer a *justification* of my moral attitudes by reasons which can be understood and accepted by others. Reason is common and public; a good reason is one which can be appreciated as such by any reasonable man. No question of criticism or justification of valuations, attitudes or proposals can arise between men except on the basis of some common ground. That common ground, in the field of moral judgements or recommendations, must be either a common aim or a common concern for one another's aims. Between men who are indifferent to each other's interests, no issue of rational justification can arise, and no reasoned discussion of preferences and policies is possible. Such men are not members of the same moral community; they are in the State of Nature as Hobbes describes it, and can only keep one another at arms' length with their weapons handy. But this is not the normal human condition. We live in communities whose members are prepared to consider one another's convenience; and between such people, rational discussion of what ought to be done is possible. Where there exists in you and me a concern for each other's welfare, and for the welfare of other persons who may be affected by our actions, I can put forward my approval of some course of action, not as a mere expression of a pro-attitude, but as something which is to the net advantage of those concerned. If it can be shown that a course of action is conducive to my happiness or satisfaction, or to yours, or to that of some third party whose welfare we are both ready to consider, this is so far a valid reason for both of us to approve that course of action. And if it can be shown that some other course of action will make a greater contribution to happiness than the first, this is so far a valid reason for preferring it to the first, regardless of our feelings about either of them. Now what actions conduce to satisfaction rather than dissatisfaction, and what actions conduce to greater satisfaction rather than less, *are* questions of fact, about which one may form true or false opinions. And the truth or falsity of such opinions is discussable. Indeed, "happiness", "satisfaction", "welfare", are vague terms. Bentham's idea that one could even in principle produce exact measures and exact calculations of quantities of happiness and misery is absurd. (One might say the same of health and disease.) But it is possible to make estimates of the likely consequences of actions in terms of happiness and misery sufficiently probable and definite to justify proposals for action. To find out what kinds of behaviour are the most favourable to human welfare is indeed very difficult, but it is not impossible to arrive at a reasonable opinion. And this is what constitutes moral rationality.

Not everybody, of course, will accept this sort of criterion of the value of actions. But in so far as it is not accepted, in so far as a disputant declares himself indifferent to the satisfaction of the persons, or some of the persons, affected by a proposed course of action, so far he withdraws from rational discussion into a declaration of his own pro- and con-attitudes – that is, into subjectivism. For objectivity in morals depends on a standard of value acceptable to all reasoners; and in this case a mutual regard for one another's satisfactions is the only basis on which agreement between all reasoners can be sought (failing the general acceptance of some one authoritative interpretation of the law of God). There *can*, then, be an examination of moral principles which we may hope will reach true conclusions about the best way of pursuing general human welfare. There can be moral authorities, namely, those people who understand better than others how human welfare can be attained. And there can be fixed and universal principles of right and wrong in so far as the conditions for attainment of human welfare are invariant; how far this is so is a question for investigation. Similarly, whether stricter or looser rules of morality are more conducive to welfare under a given set of conditions is a question of fact, on which evidence may be sought and obtained.

As for freedom of speech, we may argue for a man's right to make up his own mind on moral issues, and to express and support his opinions, in so far as these issues are matters of fact determinable by reason, and in so far as he himself accepts them as such. The principle of freedom of speech in theoretical matters is not properly invoked to protect the mendacious, the insincere or the frivolous, the malicious slanderer, the confidence trickster, the peddler of pornography, or the coiner of advertisement slogans, none of whom is trying to utter the truth. Likewise the principle of freedom of speech in moral matters can be invoked only by those who are prepared to accept the discipline of reason, the obligation to make a case. It will protect Socrates, who is prepared to state a point of view and recommend it to his fellow-citizens for their own good. It will not protect the man who scribbles abusive slogans on walls, nor the man who refuses to submit his convictions to critical discussion. (Thus it was in principle correct for the tribunals for conscientious objectors to require that every objector who wanted to be taken seriously should be required to state his reasons and submit them to critical discussion, though this bore rather hard on the inarticulate. Not that "Thus saith the Lord" or even "Thus saith the Bishop" cannot be a good reason, but "This revolts my conscience" by itself cannot.) Further, the principle of freedom of speech is not properly invoked to protect those in whom the readiness to consider the welfare of others is lacking, for this readiness is the necessary presupposition of moral discussion, and a necessary condition of membership in a moral community. Those who lack it, whether because they are infants, or because they are "moral defectives" or psychopaths, or because they exclude certain sections of the human race (Jews, negroes or infidels) from moral consideration, in so far as they do so, stand outside the moral community and outside the area of moral rationality.

Moral judgement has its source in passionate commitment; this is the truth made plain by ethical subjectivism. But it is possible to accept this truth, and still to hold that there is a vital difference between a rational moral judgement, which seeks to express the greatest possible satisfaction of the interests of those affected, and an irrational judgement which expresses merely a private attraction or repulsion. Given this distinction, we need not lose our intellectual respect for moral thinking, nor need we expel the critical assessment of actual moral standards from the purview of philosophy.

# VIII · Gains and Losses

What has been gained, and what lost, by the changes we have described? Essentially we are dealing with a change from a severer view of life which made more demands on the moral effort of the individual towards one which is gentler and less exacting, which encourages him to think that his chief wants ought to be supplied through the help of others. The principal complaint against the old-fashioned morality from which we are departing is that it was harsh. It discouraged people from enjoying themselves by insisting on putting work first and tolerating enjoyment only as the reward of work. By the severity of its demands, which were only too often beyond people's capacity, particularly that of children, it set up strains and tensions which obstructed enjoyment and led to neurosis and breakdown. Our newer morality is more relaxed and accommodating. It does not condemn a person for finding his enjoyment in his own way, even if that is not the usual way.

What we have gained is that a vast deal of avoidable misery is now being avoided. Communal provision against misfortune is enormously more effective than individual provision. Comparatively few people now go short of food and adequate shelter, of education and even of entertainment. This is only partly due to our being a much richer people – it is also partly due to a more even sharing out of such riches as there are. Comparatively few children are bullied and thwarted persistently and on principle. Comparatively few individuals have their sexual lives spoiled either by ignorance of the nature of sex or by being led to believe that sex is intrinsically shameful. Our prisons are more humane and perhaps less demoralizing places than of old.

These are great gains. At the same time they are not so great as was hoped for by many of the advocates of the change of attitude which has taken place. It is still possible to doubt whether people in general are any happier than under the old dispensation. It was hoped that with the relaxation of demands, with a gentler attitude to human imperfections, strain and tension would be reduced, far fewer people would be troubled by neurosis, *joie de vivre* would be more in evidence. The idea was that the main source of mental stress was the overstern demands made on human nature by a strict and exacting morality, and that a more permissive attitude, more tolerant of ordinary human nature, would bring about a marked reduction in neurosis. Unfortunately the evidence does not support this claim. The evidence about the incidence of mental illness shows clearly enough that even if some sources of strain have been eased, either the major strain-producing factors remain, or else they have taken new forms.

We may make one guess at the reason why the effect of a more easy-going morality is not more conspicuous. Happiness is to a large extent a function of the relation between what a person has and what he thinks he has a right to expect. He can be materially very prosperous and at the same time persistently miserable, provided that he is less prosperous than he thinks he should be. The weakness of the contemporary idea of the right to happiness, of the constant flaunting before the eyes of the citizen of all the wares which the salesmen insist he needs in order to be happy, and above all of the permissive attitude to children and the eagerness to give them what they want and allow them to do what they fancy, is that it unduly inflates expectations of what life has to offer. Magistrates in juvenile courts often comment on the bewildered mother of the young delinquent who says tearfully, "I can't understand why he went wrong – he's always had everything he wanted." A young chap sentenced for stealing a bicycle explained his behaviour in these words: "Well, I saw it leaning against a wall and I thought, 'Why should I walk?'" There is something characteristically mid-twentieth-century about his way of putting it. If people are given the impression that the fulfilment of their chief desires is something to be expected in the natural course of events, they are being let in for a good deal of disappointment. The more they expect, the harder it is to satisfy them. In the old days, when children had few possessions and little freedom, growing up was something to look forward to. But now, when children have so many possessions of their own and a great deal of freedom to please themselves, when they already stand on a footing of near-equality of importance with adults, what is there to look forward to but responsibilities for which they have not been prepared? Thus, one way and another, if our opportunities are greater, our expectations have grown along with them; and perhaps we are not much less frustrated in the end than we were at the beginning.

The changed attitude to sex must certainly have saved a good deal of unhappiness due to ignorance and prudishness. It has probably also caused a good deal of unhappiness due to people expecting far too much from sexual love. Perhaps the writers of novels and film scripts carry much of the responsibility for this. Not that they have overstated the happiness that can be derived from the right kind of marriage relationship; but they have overstated the importance of physical attraction in that relationship, and have persistently put about the idea that happiness in sexual love comes automatically as a gift, without effort. In fact the construction of a satisfying love relationship makes greater demands on one's understanding, generosity and patience than on one's sexual techniques. Love is as much an achievement of the will as it is an overflowing of the feelings; but this is rarely acknowledged in fiction. The general point is that in altering our view of happiness, from treating it as something to be earned to treating it as something one has a right to expect, in encouraging the "hire-purchase mentality" by which you first grab what you want and later on start to think about how you are going to pay for it, we have induced people to overstate their demands on life, to overestimate what can be got from it without putting very much into it.

There is another disadvantage of permissiveness, which sexual morality will also illustrate. Where there are strict rules which I, like everyone else, am expected to follow, I may find them irksome, but at least I know where I am and what I may expect. When the rules are relaxed, I know neither what other people will do nor what they expect me to do. Deciding on a course of action where there is no rule is not easier but harder than where there is a rule (even if one's decision is to break the rule). Our society seems to have reached this stage in regard to sex. The officially endorsed morality is still that of strict pre- and post-marital chastity. This is no longer generally accepted. Yet the abandoned convention has not been replaced by some other clearly understood convention, but by no convention at all. It is just not clear what is admitted and what is forbidden. Young people are left in an uncomfortable half-way position in which they are not seriously expected to live up to the old standards but are expected to pretend that they do – breaches of the rules must be done on the quiet and not openly admitted. And there are no clear notions about how much in the way of pre-marital flings or experiments, how much in the way of post-marital chopping and changing is regarded as within the bounds of decency.

This point can be generalized. The mixed-up kid is often mixed up because he is not clear what the rules are and how seriously they are to be taken. Thus neuroses of frustration are replaced by neuroses of bewilderment.

The aesthetic parallel is relevant here. Many critics of the arts have made the point that in order to get the best out of the innate talents of an artist, he must first be given a thorough *dogmatic* training – he must be taught to write, paint or compose according to pretty strict rules of some accepted style, even in a careful imitation of one particular master. Later, an artist of outstanding ability will modify the rules he has learned and work out his own personal style. But he could not have done this without the foundation given him by his earlier practice in obedient imitation.

The same is true of morality. A person who has been well trained in a given system of morality can later on modify his views, perhaps profoundly, and frame his own personal moral system. But if he has had no systematic moral guidance, if he has not first learned to imitate uncritically some model of right conduct, he will never acquire the critical judgement needed to work out his own set of principles; he just won't have the basic notions and the basic skills. This is why the effects of relaxation of standards do not show themselves in the first generation, which learned moral insight from its stricter parents, but in the second, which did not. Given a clear and firm set of moral standards a man can critically determine his own attitude to them and introduce such modifications as his own practised moral judgement suggests. But given no such clear set of standards, the task of constructing a code of conduct for himself is altogether too much for him. A vague and general goodwill is no adequate substitute for definite moral principles.

A community in which there is a sufficient supply of kindness, mercifulness, friendliness, but no settled conventions about the modes of conduct in which these sentiments are to be expressed, runs risks of two kinds. There is the risk of insecurity, because where rules and customs are loose, one never quite knows what other people are going to do, how they will interpret their obligations, up to what point they can be trusted. And there is a second sort of risk of particular concern in the present age of mass propaganda – the risk of susceptibility to manipulation. People with mere general good intentions and no definite notions as to the right way of expressing them are the easy prey of the skilful and powerful publicists, able to exhibit Big Brother's policies in an attractive light. Against the constant pressure of suggestion projecting a favourable image of the party in power, which attaches to itself the listener's diffuse and floating goodwill, the only safeguard is principle – a strong and definite conviction about what actions are right and what are wrong. Of all those classes of people whom Hitler tried to persuade and coerce, those who held out against him most firmly were Jehovah's Witnesses, whose opinions, however perverse one may think them, were at any rate definite and firm. We need clear, firm notions of good and evil to stand up against the manipulators of opinion. The slackening and blurring of our moral convictions has rendered us less resistant to persuasion.

This indefiniteness of contemporary standards is reflected in the quality of the discontent expressed in some of the literature of our time. There is a tone and spirit in this discontent which seems novel and peculiar, a kind of thought and feeling not indeed very common today, but to all appearances much commoner than in earlier ages, when it is difficult to find parallels at all. Kafka, Sartre, Camus express it; it is characteristic of many of the "outsiders" assembled in Colin Wilson's collection, and (to judge from the reception of that book and the sort of comments it evoked from a diversity of readers) it has a place in the experience of many of our contemporaries. Its characteristic complaint is that the world is "absurd", lacks "meaning", point or purpose. The people who lodge this complaint are not short of food, clothing, entertainment, steady jobs, companions, mistresses or any of the usual purchasable means of satisfaction; it is not that they want any specific article of goods or social status. Nor are they troubled by a sense of sin, of falling short of some clearly apprehended standard; they do not torment themselves with the fear of hellfire, as their melancholic ancestors sometimes did. Their difficulty is one of commitment, to use the existentialist term. They want a faith to live by, a cause to serve, a star to hitch their wagons to; without it they suffer from a sense of not being at home in the world, of being all dressed up with nowhere to go.

This sort of malaise is not likely to afflict people who are busy trying to make ends meet, though they may be very miserable in other ways. Nor does it afflict people who have a firm code of right and wrong. For if you have such a code, and give it priority in your life (all the more if you believe it to have a divine source), then living up to this code will give a further justification to your activities – they are given a meaning by being done in accordance with and in the service of your ideal, and this satisfaction is independent of any other success or gratification you may achieve. If you hold to the old-fashioned idea of life as a task, then you may congratulate yourself on having performed it to the best of your ability, you may think that your life is what it was *meant* to be. And this conviction can be a profound source of consolation in sorrow and failure. But if you have abandoned it, and yet lack the sunny disposition which would allow you to be carefree, the loss of this source of satisfaction is serious, and can be devastating. Those are still worse off who keep something of the feeling that life is a task, but have no definite notion what the task is, and so cannot tell whether they have succeeded in it – a state of mind portrayed by Kafka.

There is in man a spirit which will not let him be content with the life of the lotus-eaters. There are people who can be satisfied with a life of eating, love-making and lying in the sun; but there are also great numbers who cannot, and these include all the outstanding men, the leaders, seers and artists, as well as the wreckers. Many of us, perhaps most of us, demand that life should not merely be comfortable and convenient, but also that it should be in some more exalted fashion *justified* – even that it should be justified rather than that it should be comfortable or convenient. Nothing in human history is more striking than the way in which, whenever life threatens to become easy or simple, men devise fresh ways of making it difficult, complicated and arduous. We want to be hacking our way up ice-covered mountains when we might be lounging on the beach. We want to be picking bloody quarrels over odd words in our sacred texts when we might be joining hands in divine service. Even when we love and are loved, we peck and probe to assure ourselves that this love affair is not merely an agreeable human relationship, but a flawless fusion of minds in eternal devotion – which it cannot be.

Different views may be taken of this propensity in human nature. The devout will say that the perpetual dissatisfaction with earthly things is a mark of our participation in the divine: in the end no earthly joys content us because we are destined for the profounder joys of heaven. The beasts are content to be fed and warmed because that is the limit of their capacity for pleasure. *We* are never quite satisfied because we are always seeking the eternal and transcendent, and the greatest of the satisfactions we do attain are not those which gratify our animal appetites but those that give us glimpses of the eternal and transcendent.

Unbelievers will explain the facts otherwise. The longing for something superhuman, for the crock of gold at the foot of the rainbow, is not common to all men, and not frequent in all cultures. Probably we are not born like this, but made so. Probably the idea that simple straightforward enjoyment of food, drink, fresh air, sex and pleasant tunes is not enough to make life worth while, the idea that it requires a further justification beyond being agreeable, is one instilled into us by our elders and neighbours. We are trained to look to others to approve what we achieve in our work, and to endorse the propriety of our enjoyment of leisure, and so we grow up in the habit of expecting some sanction for our work over and above its utility, some sanction to our amusements over and above their pleasantness. We are encouraged to strive for distinction so as to win the respect of our fellows, until the craving for being and doing something out of the ordinary grows into an independent force in our personalities.

It is not necessary to decide between these and other explanations of the justification-seeking tendency in human nature. If it is inborn, we shall not get rid of it, nor if it is a consequence of social prompting, though we may contrive to reduce its strength. For our twentieth-century society, if it is to survive as a rich and technically complex society, has to be very highly disciplined. If we want a high standard of living, we must somehow persuade people to restrain many of their spontaneous tendencies, to do things they do not like and see no point in doing, to work and even to play by numbers. The "absurdity" which some existentialist philosophers find in our lives is largely the product of elaborate social organization. If people are to spend much of their time obeying somebody's orders, or working according to the impersonal rules of an organization, and if they are to do so contentedly and readily, then they must act largely for the sake of satisfactions which come from the imagination. They must be talked into, or talk themselves into, finding sense and purpose in an artificial manner of life which does not make immediate sense on the surface, in the way that the life of primitive hunters does. For many of the activities of a highly organized industrial society are prima facie pointless, and hardly any of them can be spontaneous.

In such a world, an attitude of unsophisticated, unreflective naturalness cannot survive. Only two attitudes are tolerable: either one passes one's days half-awake, half-engaged, taking nothing very seriously, moving indifferently with the rest of the crowd; or one finds a meaning and value in one's life which do not lie patent on its surface, but can only be apprehended through an interpretative effort of the understanding and the sympathies.

The need for a meaning or justification of life can be dispensed with under three conditions. Firstly, when life is perpetually interesting and agreeable, and contains nothing irksome or boring. Secondly, when the irksome or boring incidents in it have an immediate and obvious relevance and utility, as when the hunter knows that he must wearily pursue the prey if he and his kin are to eat. Thirdly, when he who endures is too stupid to question the source and value of what he endures, or to understand any explanation. Very few contemporary Englishmen are in any of these situations. There is therefore a need to be fulfilled which we suspect the old morality fulfilled somewhat better than the new: the need for something to aspire to. We are now in a position to see why the enjoyment and appreciation of life is not necessarily increased by removing difficulties, multiplying possessions and expanding opportunities for entertainment. The foundation for happiness is zest; and what most arouses zest in human beings is the effective exercise of strength, skill and foresight in response to challenge. Now the old morality, which presented life as a task, encouraged aspiration and endeavour and urged men to seek their satisfaction therein. We think it fair to say that the new morality encourages them instead to look for easy ways out.

Let us now try to discern the lineaments of the ideal man and citizen as this new morality presents him. His especial aim in life is to keep up with the Joneses and get on with the boys. His outstanding virtue is that he doesn't make trouble. He is directed towards a suitable station in life, and does his best to fit himself into it. He is friendly, adaptable, good-tempered; he has a smile for everybody, and a passion for nobody and nothing. He takes things as they come, confident that the Organization will see that he receives what he needs. He can easily transfer himself from one place or job to another. He strives to rise in the world, but does not openly display aggressiveness. He is eager to have all the latest gadgets, all the newest products of the industrial designers' ingenuity. He is never out of date. He spends freely and so helps to promote full employment and full production. He lives in the open, without reticence. He has nothing to conceal; anybody can drop in at any time. He has no extreme or unusual opinions; he has indeed no very strong opinions at all. For to disagree profoundly with the common view on politics, or religion, or films, or even what to have for breakfast, would be presumptuous and embarrassing to his companions. He is polite to eccentrics who don't go with the crowd, but he avoids their company. He has a large fund of miscellaneous information, but he knows that Metaphysics is a rude word. He cannot think of anything that would be worth dying for.

The tendency to regard this sort of personality as our ideal is not the result of a philosophical conviction that this is the best kind of man we may hope for. It is a response to demand; the demand of machine industry for docile, unenterprising, easy-going machine-tenders; the demand of bureaucratic organization for good committee-men who are adaptable and co-operative, well informed but not opinionated; the demand of the mass market for customers who spend regularly but without critical discrimination (except that between this year's model and last year's), who buy as they are told and do not think of complaining if the goods are unsatisfactory; the demand of politicians for voters who will loyally support their party and its policies without making much effort to understand them, so that one side cries "Vote Conservative – you never had it so good!" while the other says "Vote Labour and enjoy life!", both in effect saying, "Leave it to us and we will see you all right".

If this is the current ideal, what is to be said against it? It lacks aspiration and devotion. It leaves no room for those profounder experiences of artist, intellectual, explorer and saint which go so far towards justifying human existence. Indeed, it makes no demands that would force even the ordinary person to his own highest levels of interest and achievement. Instead it favours a superficial and diffused interest, shallow and second-hand emotions, according to a ready-made pattern. It stresses the satisfactions to be gained from material objects functioning as tools or as status-symbols, and underemphasizes the appreciation of persons as individuals. So, while a ready and uncritical acquiescence is gained for the decisions of leaders or for the current fashion, respect is accorded to hardly anything or anyone – not even to oneself. For self-respect is based on having one's own standards and aims and pursuing them wholeheartedly, and respect for others is based on appreciation of the same in them.

The way to get the most out of life is not to follow the fashion or take the easiest way out. (Nor is it the way of the beatniks, who abandon everything for the sake of an intense thrill, though their protest is a testimony to the general shallowness of contemporary living.) The only life worth living is that lived in the fullest possible awareness and commitment. Its follower is free in the sense of having his impulses at his own command for the pursuit of what he reflectively judges most worth while. He is always alert for beauty or wit to be appreciated, knowledge to be grasped, friends to be loved. None of this can be achieved without self-discipline and self-forgetfulness. It is on people who live at this level that we rely for our poetry and philosophy, for leadership, innovation, and that reasoned criticism of its customs without which no society can flourish and which the ideal of bland conformism discourages. But the search for one's own good life is also everyone's adventure, not to be lightly abandoned. It seems a pity to drowse one's way through life and die without having stretched oneself to the utmost.

# IX · Education and the Intellectual Ideal

There are many influences in our culture which favour the irresponsible approach, the manner of life in which men evade deep feeling or deep thinking, pass on to other persons or organizations the responsibility for their actions, exert little self-discipline, take for their leisure occupations whatever requires the least activity of mind. The irresponsible approach is encouraged by large-scale organization, by the dominance of the machine, by mass selling and advertisement, mass entertainment and propaganda. Where are we to look for countervailing influences?

The obvious and familiar answer to this question is Education, meaning by this not the whole process of human learning, but that part of it which takes places in schools and other teaching institutions. Those of our contemporaries who are anxious about the laxity and shoddiness of standards and dissatisfied with the Standard of Living as the chief end of life look to the teachers to instil into children the power and habit of self-discipline and to send into the world young people oriented towards a responsible and creative style of living. But are not the schools already doing what they can to achieve this aim? Are not the teachers committed to the values of Christian morality, of intellectual and aesthetic alertness, of discipline and civic responsibility? If the results disappoint those who rely on education to achieve these ideals, why is this so?

For one thing, too much is expected of schooling. The teacher in the classroom is very well placed for conveying information and imparting the simpler skills, and not badly placed for inculcating a fair degree of habitual orderliness, industriousness and obedience in her pupils. But she is poorly placed for making them kinder, braver, more honest or more self-reliant. Dealing with children in large groups, she can easily evoke imitation but only with difficulty arouse initiative. In the classroom, where children are mostly carrying out instructions, the situations which are critical for the development of moral character rarely arise. For inculcation of moral standards, the teacher has to depend largely on the unreliable influence of talk.

Her own example can indeed be powerful; but inspiring teachers are none too common, and we cannot expect this spiritual grace to be communicated by training-college courses. The strongest influences of habit and example still belong to the out-of-school environment, and the parents are vastly more important here than the teachers. Those parents who hand over to the schools the responsibility for the moral training of their children, and those teachers who claim this responsibility for themselves, are dangerously mistaken.

For another thing, the school is only one influence among many. The voice of the telly or the advertisements may speak louder and with a greater power to fascinate. Teachers, in relation to their older pupils, stand as representatives of the previous generation, the old-fashioned, the square; young people reach maturity and self-confidence in part by developing their own ways of behaving in conscious opposition to them.

(It was no different in nineteenth-century public schools.) Even in the adult world, the teachers carry no great prestige. Measured by the accepted standard of income, they are poorly regarded by the community at large in comparison with salesmen, politicians and entertainers. They no longer command a near-monopoly of educated female talent. They have been deprived of the power to intimidate, and they have few resources of status or glamour to impress themselves and their ideas upon their charges. Thus they cannot effectively propagate ideals and standards without the support of the outside world. They can of course successfully convey such values as are accepted by the society for which their pupils are being prepared, for they can point to the recognition and rewards given by society to those who accept and achieve these values. But wherever the values of the school seem to be different from those of the outside world, it is the outside world which usually exercises the stronger influence in the long run. The sharp separation between learning and doing does indeed make the school a very different place from the world of manufacture, commerce and administration, which is dominated by other patterns of behaviour, other ideals, risks and opportunities than those to be found in the classroom. The scholastic curriculum often appears irrelevant to the serious concerns of working life, for which the teachers (whose lives have been lived mostly in schools), seem ill-equipped to give adequate guidance. In these circumstances it is naïve to expect teachers to convey to children values to which the rest of society is indifferent. In the past, indeed, the Church had some success in this endeavour. But the Church had a unified faith, an explicit and agreed set of beliefs and models of behaviour along with spiritual incentives and sanctions. The secular educational system has none of these resources. And even if it had, what overriding scheme of values could it advocate except that handed down by its master, the State?

There is, all the same, one kind of moral ideal which the teachers can aim at propagating with some hope of success, because they have backing from the outside world. This is the ideal of the scientific intellectual. Our age is distinguished from all past ages by the extent of available knowledge and the complexity of institutions. It is an age of science and of planning, in which complex structures of theoretical knowledge are employed to organize masses of material and masses of people for the fulfilment of complex large-scale projects. Therefore a role of vital and increasing importance is played by the scientific intellectual. Leadership in modern society devolves on those who can master the scientific information and devise the intricate plans for a monster factory, a hospital, a metropolitan traffic system, a European Economic Community. Increasingly, men and nations are made prosperous and powerful by scientific knowledge and technical skill. Those who possess this knowledge, having in their hands the sources of power and prosperity, are coming to possess prestige and influence. It is now very hard, and is becoming harder, to get accepted for a position involving responsibility and power without being able to produce the appropriate certificates of book or laboratory learning. The upper classes of the next generation are being selected primarily by competitive examination; those who get through their examinations go on to occupy the superior posts, those who do not become the hewers of wood and drawers of water. And in these examinations the scientific and technical subjects continue to gain in importance over the arts subjects. The spirit of our age is already largely scientific and likely to become more so. Ruling classes of the past were often distinguished by traditional behaviour patterns: people acquired the aristocratic point of view by imitation of certain habits and development of appropriate sentiments, so that their rejection of vulgarity came to seem instinctive. But the modern scientist, technocrat or organizer, if he is to do his job efficiently, is committed to the open mind, to the construction of novel patterns of thought and action, to the domination of understanding over intuition, feeling and habit. No process of learning by habituation will make a twentieth-century planner; he has to use his intellect, to be a master of theory, to deal by means of symbols, reports and statistics with things he cannot see or handle.

As the ruling classes of the past had their ideal types (Sir Lancelot, Sir Roger de Coverley), so there is an Ideal Egghead, depicted by many generations of eggheads from Plato onwards. He is sincere in facing facts, devoted to truth; he refuses to distort his beliefs to accord with his desires; he avoids pretence or humbug; he rejects superstition (that is, the acceptance of ideas and practices sanctioned by traditional authority without adequate evidence of their validity). He is ready to meet all his fellow men on the level ground of rational discussion, in which there is no class, race or sex prejudice, but everybody who talks is entitled to a hearing and every suggestion is considered according to its merits and not according to the source from which it comes. He has faith in the capacity of men to achieve a mastery of their environment, and, still more important, of their own wayward selves. Outside his professional concerns, the scientifically or philosophically minded man is above all the man who knows what he is doing and why. He will try to keep his head, to plan his actions, to be a critical and discriminating buyer, voter or patron of the arts. Political problems he will handle like laboratory problems, detachedly and objectively, treating government as the art of resolving human difficulties and not as the defence of some absolute right of nationality, creed or class. An ideal of this kind comprises some of the elements missing from the alternative contemporary ideal we sketched above – aspiration, self-discipline, freedom. As for intensity of experience, it is only to those who have not lived it that the intellectual life seems pallid in its emotions and satisfactions.

Is this an adequate ideal for future generations? Does it supply us with something to admire and aspire to, capable of giving inspiration and justification to life? As far as concerns the men and women of higher intelligence, those who can get through their examinations and make their way to positions of importance, the answer is Yes. There is enough in the life lived in mastering theoretical, technical and organizational problems, in setting knowledge to work for the betterment of the human condition, in multiplying the material equipment, improving the health, and extending the co-operation of the human species, to make life seem purposive and self-discipline worth while.

But for those who fail their examinations, the outlook is more doubtful. We can, indeed, argue that the scientific attitude is as desirable for the underlings in modern society as for their overlords, and for the same reasons. In past ages a man's adaptation to his environment could take place largely through the development of half-conscious habits, ways of thinking and feeling, judging and responding, which he picked up from other people without having to ponder much about them. Education could consist in learning a craft by following a craftsman about on the job and picking up his habits. But this style of learning one's way about the world is no longer adequate; if it were, we should not be worrying about declining standards. The method will work only if the environment to which people must adapt themselves remains fairly constant. In our time, environments do not remain constant, but change continually, drastically and unpredictably, and so we have to be able to adapt ourselves to a perpetual changeableness in the circumstances of our existence. The faculty whereby man adapts himself to changing circumstances is the intellect; consequently the development of the intellect in ordinary men is urgent now as it has never been before. Those who do not understand what is happening to them, who cannot with critical alertness size up new situations as they come along, are bound to be pushed around by circumstances and by the men who do understand. Thus the egghead mentality is something of which all citizens stand in some need. They need technical, biological and sociological information to give them some grasp of the programmes of action based on this information. They also need the attitude to life of the scientifically-minded man, the man who tries all the time to understand what he is doing and why, and acts not from habit nor from instinct, nor because this is what has always been done, nor because it is the latest fashion, nor because he has been told to do it in an impressive tone of voice by some supposedly authoritative person, but because he sees some good reason for doing this rather than some other thing.

But though it may be desirable to have a philosophic people and not just a philosophic aristocracy, is this a feasible idea? Is there not a limit set by innate intelligence and temperament which will prevent large numbers of people from even understanding the scientific point of view? Are there not "slaves by nature", from whom it is hopeless to expect more than passive participation in modern civilization, to whom thinking is painful, responsibility a burden and aesthetic appreciation limited to cinerama and pop-songs? Up to a point, such people are ready to admire eggheads and admit their utility. But dislike and distrust of the intellectual are deep rooted among the common people . . . rooted in the inability of the unintellectual person to share the point of view of the intellectual. Anyone can imagine what it was like to discover a new continent, but few can enter into the experience of those who now make scientific advances. Nothing cuts a man off so effectively from his working-class or petty-bourgeois friends and relations as a university education. To get the general public interested in intellectually eminent persons it is necessary to talk about their personalities, hobbies, pets, houses – anything except their work. Doubtless, this gap between those who can and those who cannot grasp the intellectual point of view is partly a matter of innate ability.

Our present educational system emphasizes and widens this gap. In so far as we accept the principle that intellectual ability shall be the qualification for eminence we lay upon the schools the task of selecting the ruling class of the future. (This task does not always fit in very well with strictly educational aims. It is difficult to devise an examination system which does not put the critical and wide-ranging mind at a disadvantage compared with the crammed and limited mind, and so incite the teachers to cram.) Thus the division between grammar, technical and secondary modern schools foreshadows distinct social classes of Guardians, Auxiliaries and Craftsmen in the Platonic manner, the proportions of these classes being determined, not by the distribution of ability among children, but by the number of school places available, which may or may not be well adapted to society's needs. In the contest to become candidates for the most desirable jobs, the great majority are bound to be losers. The senior classes of our secondary modern schools contain large numbers of unreceptive and resentful pupils who have rejected the scholastic ideal put before them – some because they would under any conditions be unreceptive to intellectual training, some because they are told they are not very good at scholastic subjects and wish to waste no more time and effort on them, some because they see no adequate connection between what they are set to learn and what they want to do with their lives thereafter. The longer these children are kept at school (especially in these days of early physical maturity) the more discontented and delinquent they become, and the more risk there is that they will infect the whole system with their disaffection. Those who say that young people need more education are probably right. But it is doubtful whether a further period of compulsory schooling, involving a still longer delay to their entry into the world of workers and earners, is the most suitable way of providing them with it. It might in the end be better to offer generous facilities for learning to those who demand them, at the time of life when they have come to feel the need, which is not in every case in the 'teens. The sort of education which would be most valuable to the less intellectual children would be one associated much more closely with their working lives and their actual leisure activities. Perhaps this education should run alongside working life instead of finishing just at the point where the young people have serious problems to tackle and serious questions to ask. It should concern itself with the choice of consumer goods and the development of taste in dress or popular music, beginning with their existing tastes and encouraging them to discuss these critically and increase their range of appreciation. Other suitable features of the curriculum would include the economics of hire-purchase, household budgeting, child-rearing and personal relations in industry and the home. The method of presentation should be one of discussion rather than instruction from the rostrum, as in the education of university students. This type of education could be clearly seen as useful to the students and not merely designed to keep them temporarily out of mischief.

A meritocratic system, in which superior status is based on intellectual achievement, can claim to be juster than systems in which it is based on inheritance. But it does not follow that meritocratic class distinctions would arouse less class resentment among the lower orders. The ancient aristocracies of birth and wealth, segregated from infancy and trained to cultivate marks of differentiation from the common people, could keep up a show of being intrinsically different from others. But this is no longer possible when the segregation takes place by means of an examination taken by everybody at about the age of eleven. The boy next door who has merely been sharp enough to pass a test which his neighbours have failed excites in them no awe, little admiration, often a good deal of resentment. The losers in this competition for advancement may well be reluctant to admire their successful rivals and to accept their standards and values.

Thus we demand too much of our schools if we require them to assume the main responsibility for instilling moral values. Their capacity to do this is limited by competition from other sources of influence, often with greater prestige and persuasive power than the school-teachers, and by the resistance of their less scholarly pupils to the values of a system which segregates them as inferiors.

# X · The Uses of Leisure

We have suggested that one condition of happiness, at least for many people, is to have something that they can do whole-heartedly, some activity or aim in which they can fulfil themselves. An outstanding characteristic of the modern attitude to life is the extent to which such fulfilment is being sought in leisure activities rather than in work. Work can be sufficiently satisfying for a man to give his whole heart to it either if it is itself absorbing as an exercise of strength, skill or ingenuity, or if the work a man does is his own enterprise done under his own direction and for his own profit. Two contemporary developments make it harder for men to make their work their life. On the one hand there is an increasing tendency to reduce the operations of workers to routines, so that a man employs the same movements hour after hour, week after week, movements dictated by the pace and construction of a machine and by the time-and-motion study experts. Not everybody dislikes repetitive work; plenty of people prefer it; but *nobody can be wrapped up in it*. (Indeed one ground for preferring it is that it leaves some attention over for daydreaming and thinking about other things.) On the other hand independent men who work for themselves under their own direction and for their own profit are becoming steadily scarcer. It is possible to be devoted to a craft or a profession, to a master or leader, or to the increase of one's bank balance; but it is hardly possible to be devoted either to repetitive work or to one's role in a big organization (unless it is a role of exceptional importance). Few today have intrinsically satisfying work; even fewer are their own masters.

At the same time the very processes which have made so much work mechanical and servile have also enabled men to shorten that part of their lives that must be given to it. And the same technological advance which has produced leisure for us has also provided us with a hitherto undreamed-of range of occupations and entertainments to fill it. Sport now takes dozens of forms suitable to diverse climates and geographical features, and most of these activities are now open to every physically fit member of the western communities. Travel for pleasure both inside one's own country and abroad has since the war become progressively easier on account of increased hotel accommodation and the development of every kind of transport. Like sport, travel has come within the reach of the masses; travel agencies have energetically tackled the problem of organizing tours for parties and for individuals and their advertisements fill entire pages of the newspapers and weeklies. The individual pleasure motorists of Britain at the height of the holiday season clog the country's roads and overflow its parking spaces. Facilities for hobbies such as gardening, photography, flower arrangement, tape-recording, bridge, and make-it-yourself, fill departments of the stores, while books, periodicals and broadcast programmes all advise the enthusiast on the techniques of his interest. Almost every kind of book can be more cheaply bought as a paperback. For the man who likes paintings the range of more or less adequate reproductions increases year by year. And for the music lover the concert hall is supplemented by gramophone records and tapes which on the better reproducing machines provide convincing renderings of a wide variety of compositions that he might seldom have the opportunity to hear in a live performance. All this in addition to the offerings of mass entertainment. We have both the leisure time and the means of filling it. Mechanization and Organization, while depriving us of much of the interest of our work, pay back by offering us a marvellous range of things to do as soon as we clock out.

Clocking out itself is the symbol of an uncommonly sharp separation between work and leisure. The things a man does when he is not working are normally quite different from and unconnected with those he does on the job. He is in a different place, often many miles away; he is usually among different people; hardly anything links leisure with work, so that his life is divided into two contrasted parts. Increasingly the work comes to be regarded as a necessary nuisance for the sake of the leisure; it is viewed principally as a source of income, very little as a source of satisfaction. The typical school leaver interviewed by the Youth Employment Officer shows great interest in rates of pay, not much in the operations he will have to perform, none whatever in the ultimate social purposes of those operations. So we have an increasing tendency for people to seek the main interest of their lives in leisure interests. At one social and cultural level there is the shop assistant who gets through her tasks with a minimum expenditure of energy so that she can really let herself go in dancing, skating, cinema-going or necking, or the workman whose sole topic of conversation for eight months of the year is football. At another level there is a very common inclination to regard the appreciation of works of art as the supreme value in life – an activity clearly separate from that other part of one's existence in which one earns a living in the ugly, philistine, workaday world. People no longer listen to the preaching of the Victorian gospel of the sanctity of work and the iniquity of amusements.

(That gospel is still zealously preached by communist parties in the poorer countries in which they flourish, where, without recognizing it, they fill a similar historical role to that of the nineteenth-century *bourgeoisie* whom they abhor.) A negative attitude to work, treating it purely as a source of gain and not at all as a source of interest, is widespread amongst our working classes, whose jobs tend to give small opportunity for absorption in the process or pride in the result. Very many of them seem unconcerned with the quality of their output, resistant to attempts to increase efficiency (unless the whole benefit of such increases goes to raise their wages), ready to abandon their posts for the sake of trivial squabbles with little regard for the injuries done to their fellow workers or the general public. The job is to them only a way of earning money, and their main interest in life lies elsewhere.

This valuing of leisure above work is of course nothing new. The general opinion at most periods of history has been that work is a curse laid on the children of Adam for his and their sins, and to live the good life a man needs plenty of leisure and plenty of money. Plato and Aristotle assure us that labourers and domestic servants are incapable of the Good Life; and aristocracies have always taken it as a disgrace to have to work for a living. Even our Puritan ancestors, who were uncommonly struck on work for its own sake, looked forward to a heaven in which there was none. Our society is not therefore peculiar in valuing leisure above work, but only in the quantity of leisure and resources for filling it which are at the disposal of ordinary people. The problem of how to fill in time, how to choose between many possible spare-time occupations, which used to concern only the well-to-do, now concerns most English people who are not parents of young children.

Yet many restrict themselves to a curiously limited selection of these. Watching television accounts for the bulk of the spare time of large numbers in almost every age group except the courting group. Another popular pastime is watching sport, whether directly or by television. Gambling still takes up a good deal of the leisure of adults. This includes filling in pools coupons, betting on races, studying form and attending race meetings, playing card games for money, dicing, gambling on machines, and the recent bingo craze, which has filled large halls with enthusiasts feverishly listening for the number that will enable them to win. It is not easy to decide whether the widespread spare-time pursuits of gardening, interior decoration and domestic do-it-yourself should count as work or as play, since they are often undertaken with the sole object of economizing on expenditure, yet many people undoubtedly engage in them for their own sake. Sheer loafing, especially in public houses, seems to have declined somewhat since the war, probably because most can now afford to gamble or watch television instead, and many do their own decorating.

Now among the pastimes listed here as common, home and garden maintenance are the only ones involving full activity, and gambling is an intermediate pursuit involving a minimum of activity in the selection of a fancy to be backed. Loafing, watching sport and televiewing are purely passive uses of leisure, television being the most time-consuming of those on record.

When we compare these popular pastimes with those of the early 1900s we are struck with the far greater passivity of present-day people at their play. The movement towards greater passivity began with the cinema and sound broadcasting. Our grandparents, and even some of our parents before those innovations, filled their spare time with doing rather than with listening or looking on. They played games as well as watching them, they sang and played on the much abused piano, and winter evenings were taken up with fine sewing, crocheting, fretwork, card-playing for counters, chess and, for the less intellectual, draughts, halma and ludo. Most women, if they did not make their own clothes, at least trimmed hats. Hat-trimming is a creative activity which could easily be by-passed by the use of a plain ribbon band. But this would not have contented our mothers and their friends in the early 1900s; they liked to load their wide-brimmed straws and covered buckram "shapes" with fruits and flowers, feathers or even entire birds, renewed each season according to the fantasy of the artificer. Almost every respectable girl awaiting marriage filled her bottom drawer with handstitched linen, a dozen of everything. Jams, pickles and cakes were usually made at home; "shop cake" was blushed for. Women invited one another to tea to taste the latest culinary triumphs. And all these crafts were pursued with such gusto! From our own childhoods we can recall little of the sitting with hands unoccupied that is normal in the present-day television-dominated living-room.

What makes the modern addiction to passive amusements the more surprising is that many people now work for their wages upwards of fifteen hours a week less than their predecessors sixty years ago and so must have more spare time, even allowing for protracted journeys to work. Further, they are better fed and doctored, and so might be expected to have more surplus energy. It is a strange state of affairs. By increased mechanization we have deprived many of all their satisfaction in the job, but on the credit side we have increased their hours of free time. Yet that credit item is all too often squandered on mere spectatorship, frequently of things little worthy of attention. This raises the question whether there is anything wrong with such passive use of leisure (especially when each day there are several hours of it preceded by work not itself exhausting).

Let us take a glance at the daily life of Mrs Jones, a not-untypical housewife whose children have reached school age and who therefore is free to enjoy running her home without distraction during at least five days of the week. Is she contented? She is not. She has tried going out to work again but given it up as too tiring in addition to the domestic round. Yet the truth is that the house alone does not fill her life. It might if she were still genuinely interested in it, or alternatively if she had formed the habit of doing wholeheartedly anything that happened to come her way. As it is, whenever her domestic duties allow (and sometimes when they should not!) she sits down in front of the television set and lets it take charge of her emotional life. If there is nothing attractive on the "telly" she turns the pages of a magazine and perhaps begins to read a "romance". In between the viewing and the magazine perusal, while washing up, cooking and plying the vacuum-cleaner, she pursues daydreams based on material culled from magazine or television programmes. Light background music from the sound radio provides a fitting accompaniment. Children and husband eventually come home and have to be fed. Afterwards she may spend the remainder of the evening with the telly again, in her own home or someone else's. At the week-end if it is fine the family may go out in their car; but to keep up the stimulation she can no longer do without, she wants the car radio switched on. At the end of the day she feels restless and at the same time flat. She cannot sleep without a tranquillizer, and the following morning a pep tablet will be needed to get her moving. She exists in an almost incessant round of titillation, leading inevitably to emotional exhaustion, without anywhere the relief of full satisfaction. The outcome is an unfocused discontent, begetting reliance on yet more thrills, tranquillizers and pep pills. And there are many men and women on repetition jobs whose lives present variations of this pattern.

But what is the effect of an exclusive mental diet of television and the popular Press? Will not its victims come to see life in terms of their entertainments, and become obsessed with getting "their share" of the things so temptingly advertised? Don't they begin to value themselves and their friends according to the numbers, cost and up-to-dateness of material possessions? Isn't there the risk that their chief objective in life will become The Thrill, and their one aversion boredom? What happens to their zest for ordinary day-to-day living?

There is of course some exaggeration in this account. But the writer of this passage once passed ten years in the manner described, and honestly judges that the years so spent were wasted years during which she failed to grow up. And this is our chief ground for discontent with the exclusively passive use of leisure in onlooking of various kinds: that it retards the development of its addicts because instead of trying out activities for themselves and so learning, adjusting and maturing, they are wasting the years in a dream of identification with models who are often frivolous and sometimes anti-social.

A feature of this way of life is the practice of half-attention. Half-attention is already encouraged by repetition work in home and factory. Then the repetition-worker clocks out or reaches the end of the chore, and goes on paying only half of his attention to whatever is done during leisure. The layouts of the tabloid Press, like advertisements, are designed to catch and hold the eye of people who pay attention reluctantly. Urban environments are full of similar features shouting "Glance at me!" (Perhaps a good deal of urban ugliness is tolerated because few people really look.) It is assumed that violence will be needed to take hold of the wandering mind of the ordinary citizen. Wherever he is, his attention tends to be divided between its nominal object, his awareness of the people he is with (and many are never alone save when making their toilet), and his reverie. Women may well be more subject than men to this disorder, for they get more of the repetitive jobs, and child-tending naturally contributes to forming a habitually divided mind. Women also tend to be more interested than men in the impression they believe they are making on other people, and this sort of self-consciousness, too, plays a big part in the growth of the half-attention habit. Gradually, full attention steadily maintained over a long period is becoming exceptional for the average citizen in our civilization. He is only partly aware of what is going on around him, only marginally interested in it. There are many things that he "knows" only in a ramshackle fashion. To reassure himself he collects *faits divers*, as a jackdaw collects shining objects; systematic knowledge is beyond him.

But this sort of experience is a waste of life. The full harvest of living can only be reaped if complete attention is given to whatever one is about. It is not only that activity at fullest stretch gives the completest satisfaction. One must learn to concentrate awareness on the object of interest, whether this is one's own activity or that of another, a thing contemplated, another personality or oneself. The veering tendency of the human mind is so well known that yoga techniques always begin with exercises in concentration. Zen indeed aims at teaching the initiate to attend in everyday living at such a level that each moment furnishes the justification for the whole of life. But it seems that most of us will do anything sooner than live with all our heart and soul. It is so much easier to live by proxy through entertainment, and even then only to pay a partial and scattered attention to what is going on.

Yet it is idle to suppose that entertainment really gives us the gist of what it is like to do this or that, without the trouble of personal exertion. In fact it can never do more than convey a hint. If you doubt this, try to recollect the shock with which you first saw some place despite your familiarity with photographs of it, even in colour. Neither photographs, films nor descriptions had succeeded in preparing me for the impact of Venice, when I first descended those broad shallow steps from the railway station and stood on the steamer landing pontoon, digesting the fact that this really was a city whose streets were paved with water. The dance of the light reflected from waves on the undersides of bridges, the oddly assorted crowds unharried by wheeled traffic that thronged piazza and alley, the enlivening sea breeze as one emerges from some ravine in the centuries-old masonry, the warmth of the sun still held in the walls after dusk as the witness of summer's completeness, the faded sumptuousness of St Mark's, beautiful things side by side with junk heaped up in shop windows, all sparkling and glowing with colour like Aladdin's cave, how could the wiliest entertainer communicate this sensuous feast to a passive audience who have not shared the experience in person?

Again, the man who sits in an arm-chair watching the film of the first ascent of Everest is not even so near to the experience of those who made that ascent as the rough note on the back of an envelope is to the finished painting. For the spectator of the film usually has no conception of the sensation of physical fitness that is a concomitant of being ready to climb an exacting mountain, does not know how rock feels to the touch when wet or when frosted, cannot imagine the muscular sensations of changing one's grip in a tricky place, knows nothing of the climber's rhythm of movement or his deep relaxation in repose.

Neither in art nor in entertainment is there any substitute for reality, yet it is widely supposed that anyone can escape from his own monotonous or frustrated existence to a fuller life by identifying himself with fictitious figures or by responding to the titillations of entertainment. He does indeed escape, but not into a fuller life; it is into debilitating fantasy that he escapes, which leaves him unfitter for the satisfying life he craves.

The passive uses of leisure might indeed do little harm if they were always balanced by activities. Unfortunately inertia is a habit difficult to shake off. An hour before the television set easily becomes an evening wasted. When this happens day after day alongside a job felt to be intrinsically unrewarding, is such a life being lived as completely as it might be? The scope of the ordinary person in Britain today is far wider than that of his grandparents. Is spectatorship the best use he can make of it?

It is often claimed that certain broadcast programmes widen the interests and increase the general knowledge of their audiences. If this were so, we should expect to find enormously increased issues of non-fiction books from the public libraries and long queues registering for adult education classes of the non-vocational type. So far few such phenomena have been observed. The interest stimulated by even the best broadcast programmes is plainly insufficient to modify the behaviour of more than a small fraction of their audiences. Such programmes, like other kinds of mass-communication, tend to arouse a lively passing interest and then be quickly forgotten. It may be that this arousing, day in day out, of dozens of interests that are never followed up, is positively harmful in that it fritters away the attentiveness of the viewer and atrophies his resolution.

The common argument in favour of the present emphasis on entertainment is that people should be given what they want. What they want, as shown by viewing statistics and the circulations of magazines and dailies, is with few exceptions the frivolous and the sensational, the over-emphatic, and whatever makes immediate appeal to uncultivated tastes and unschooled minds, whatever makes little demand on the energies and discrimination of the consumer. In general, popular taste is undeveloped taste. Many of the habits, attitudes and values of the English today are really juvenile: for instance, the cult of The Thrill (which is proper to adolescence when we are experimenting with our emotions), and the commercially stimulated crazes for pop-singers, bingo and ten-pin bowling, stiletto heels and back-combing, poodles and budgerigars, the unpractical picture window and open-plan house, iced lollies, candy-floss and incessant cigarette smoking; and the prime value of conformism, of eagerly imitating the behaviour, speech and purchases of acquaintances. We expect these kinds of behaviour in school-children, whose individual tastes have still to be formed. It looks as though many people make no attempt to find out what they personally would do with most satisfaction, but unthinkingly follow the lead set by Jones. A less immature society would long ago have left Jones to his own devices, and devoted its energies to training young people to do and enjoy according to their individual abilities. No doubt the present-day Peter Pans of all ages are highly profitable to commercial interests. But Peter Pan is wasting his precious opportunity of living his own life, and our society spends its resources on fripperies while it is still notably deficient in educational facilities, housing and an effective transport system. Thus our wilful immaturity is detrimental both to society and individuals.

Why is our society so stubbornly immature? Why do experienced adults defer to or even ape the preferences of teenagers? – after all, the Twist is not a dance for middle-aged knees, stiletto heels and short tight skirts look appalling on most women over thirty, besides being uncomfortable, and the cult of The Exciting is childish. Yet we see people who before the war would have been adjudged "old enough to know better" enthusiastically trying to demonstrate that they too are "with it". They seem to assume that youth is not only the physical zenith of life, but in every way its peak, so that to prolong the usages of young people into middle age is to keep a hold on all that is most rewarding in human experience. Surely they are mistaken. The more subtle, like the more enduring and reliable enjoyments, require prolonged self-training and a wide range of experience; it follows that they are commoner in older people who have had time for self-preparation. But instead of preparing for the pleasures of maturity, there are many who shut their eyes and cling to the remnants of their youth, thus inevitably setting a bad example to their juniors. Perhaps they want to "remain young" because they believe that the young cannot be expected to please their elders, youth being life's climax and not to be marred by any self-restraint? It is arguable that this situation is the natural outcome of giving people what they think they want in entertainment, marketing and child-rearing. Today it is the entertainers and advertisers who play the part of moral tutors to the populace, showing them what they "ought to want" in order to "be with" the present trend. And the populace, too much under the influence of spoiled children and unconsciously coming to adopt their values, acclaims the morality of Effortless Living. But who is going to try to convince them that little satisfaction can be expected without previous effort, that passivity is a cause of boredom, that half-attention and living-by-proxy produce in the long run only apathy and disillusionment?

There is indeed in the variety of leisure activities available ample scope for a full development of human prowess and ingenuity, for achievement and distinction, for savouring life and finding it worth while. But we doubt whether spontaneous use will be made of those opportunities by a class of people without interest and without influence in the business concerns of life. For whenever a powerful minority dominates business activity it will also dominate leisure activity. If the minority consists of the leaders of an aggressive political party, then leisure activities will be commandeered in support of a political programme. The party line will become obligatory on poets and novelists, and even musicians; sport will become a military operation aimed at the defeat of the foreigner, and every club will be under the watchful eye of an agent of the party. Where it is the business men who dominate, the pressures will be of another kind. Their concern with leisure activities is to make them subservient to the commercial interest. They use culture, entertainment and sport as sources of profit, even if this involves the stifling of spontaneous interest. They turn artists into publicity men, and break into radio programmes with "commercials". They exploit the superior selling power of the trivial and superficial. They take our hobbies and amusements and transform them into profitable businesses. Football, for instance, which started as a game for ordinary chaps to amuse themselves with in their spare time, has become a large business concern in which a small number of highly skilled professionals play, a huge number of followers merely watch; and it is passing into a further stage, reached long ago by horse racing, when it will exist mainly to enable a still larger number of people quite ignorant of the game to gamble on the results of the play. When a sport becomes professionalized, when a player's skill becomes a money-making asset for him to bargain with and for his employers to buy and sell, half the fun goes out of the game.

Perhaps in an ideal community all those activities done mainly for the pleasure of doing them and not for the maintenance of life, health and comfort would be outside the money-making system altogether. It is possible to imagine a social order in which nobody would be a professional footballer, painter or entertainer; in which everybody would have to spend some moderate part of his time in necessary useful labour and thereby earn his livelihood, and for the rest could practise without payment whatever art or skill most appealed to him. Among those cultural pursuits which might be better taken out of the commercial nexus one might reckon both religion and the arts side of education. Religion is a part of culture, for the enhancement of the quality of living, not a part of economics for the maintenance of subsistence. Now that we no longer believe that our national prosperity depends on performing the prescribed religious rituals and that therefore we must hire professionals to perform them, we might be willing to treat religion as a leisure activity better pursued by volunteers than by professionals, who are required to combine the preaching of their faith with the advancement of their Church's economic interests, and whose audiences subject everything they say to the tacit discount "Ah, he's paid to say that". Similarly, the study of literature (beyond mere reading and writing), of history and philosophy and the fine arts, and perhaps of natural history and natural science in so far as they are unconnected with technology, are properly leisure pursuits, not useful studies in the way that medicine, engineering, geography and biochemistry are useful. They would perhaps be better studied if people did not make livings out of them, and have to pass examinations in them as a condition of getting jobs.

But in our society as it is, the Standard of Living, in the sense of the greatest possible quantity of goods to be manufactured and put to use, is the dominant value, the overriding social aim. If for instance it is economically advantageous for married women to work in factories, shops and offices, they do so, and some makeshift arrangement is found for looking after their children in their absence; it is assumed that the increased production of material wealth is so clearly important that one need not consider whether these makeshift arrangements are adequate for the psychological well-being of the children. If more production can be got out of machinery by operating it all round the clock, then some workers must become nocturnal animals and consort with their families only at week-ends. The beauty of the English countryside fights a manifestly losing battle against the invasion of factories, power stations, dormitories and bazaars. Of course material wealth is a means to good living, but we do suggest that the material standard of living is insufficiently inspiring to serve as a paramount aim of life, more especially at a stage in economic progress when the essential needs of all citizens can be supplied by production at the existing level.

To make the most of leisure, to make it yield satisfactions and opportunities for appreciation and achievement which working life does not yield, it would be necessary to relieve people of their subservience to the Standard of Living as a dominating goal. And why not? The idea that the multiplication of material wealth is the most important thing in life is not a necessary outcome of the ordinary human love of comfort and acquisition. The working classes have always looked somewhat askance at it. Its dominance in our society is maintained by the aid of a tremendous apparatus of persuasion whose function is to convince people of the paramount importance of possessions, to bring into existence artificial appetites that they would have been just as happy without, to make them discontented with the good things they have so that they will throw them away and buy others that are no better – all for the sake of increasing employment (that is, the total quantity of labour) and production (that is, the total quantity of manufactured articles regardless of their capacity to supply existing needs). It is hard to believe that the community as a whole would be any the worse if this whole vast and costly apparatus were dismantled, and advertisement limited to notifications of the availability and price of articles, and specification of their composition. In this sector of the struggle between freedom and servitude, the consumers' associations are doing much to make it possible for man (or more often, woman) as purchaser to behave with rationality, to know what he is doing and why.

It is then possible to conceive of a society in which work, that is the production of the material necessities of life, would be regarded as comparatively unimportant, in which men would exert and fulfil themselves principally in their leisure occupations. Yet there seems something unsatisfactory about a condition in which work is not a part of the good life, but only a preparation for it, without grace, dignity or sanctity, so that men lose interest in the activities whereby their lives are sustained, and thereby lose control over them. It is doubtful whether such a duality of attitudes could in the end be satisfactory. Man has only one personality, and the attitudes of mind he develops will show up both in his work and in his leisure activities. If during his working time he has to behave like an automaton, mechanically adjusting himself to the requirements of a machine and its programme, not understanding what he is doing or why, not having any say in the way it is done, it is unrealistic to expect the same man when off duty to change his personality and become independent, self-reliant, creative. The mass media are the natural cultural expression of the mass-production workers, and the passivity of current entertainment is the counterpart of the passivity of present-day working lives. No community of servants has ever made any substantial contribution to culture; it is the work of free men. Thus no endeavour to raise the standards of sensitivity, alertness, discrimination or inventiveness in leisure activities is likely to get very far so long as these qualities find no place in working life. The superficial, irresponsible attitude of mind will prevail unless adequate scope can be found in public life, in production and administration, for the mature and responsible attitude.

The fundamental problem is how to secure scope for individual responsibility, initiative and self-respect in a mechanized and organized society, especially in industrial life. We do not know the solution of this problem, for it has not been anybody's concern to treat it as a problem and look for a solution. Liberal theory has assumed that liberty is secure enough if the state does not itself direct production, and if there are enough enterprises in a given industry to ensure plenty of competition. Socialist theory has assumed that if everybody is an employee of the community to which he belongs, then everybody will be happy in his work, and will find in the prosperity of the whole community a sufficient incentive and interest. Both assumptions are absurd. Business management is concerned with making production profitable. Trade unions are concerned with exacting the largest possible pay packet for the shortest possible hours and with very little else. Hardly anyone is bothered by the problem of making working life satisfying and agreeable to the worker. The existing attitude is reasonable in an age of poverty when the increase of production may legitimately take precedence of all other aims, when it is better to be sweated than to starve. But our age can afford to look beyond this, and try to make working life such that in every task there is scope for the exercise of the worker's ability, for the assumption of some responsibility, for self-respect in the satisfaction of work well done. In so far as under mass-production conditions responsibility for the job cannot for technical reasons be individual, it is desirable that the individual should take his due share in collective decision and responsibility. He should at least know what he is doing and to what end, what part he plays in a common purpose. If too often the workers in our large industries behave like children, downing tools over trivialities, it is probably because they are treated like children, expected to do their jobs without bothering about the policy of the management or the purpose of the whole enterprise.

We have drawn attention to a growing passivity in the use of leisure, the more remarkable in view of the unsatisfying character of many present-day jobs. We have suggested that the half-attention and daydreaming appropriate to the performance of repetitive work have been carried over into leisure occupations, and that people without scope for adult responsibility on the job will continue to behave childishly throughout their lives.

# XI · Looking Ahead

The ethical trends we have been discussing have their source in massive transformations of our ways of living and thinking. These transformations are likely to continue in the same direction. It is therefore to be expected that the consequent changes in morals have by no means reached their limit but will be carried further. Indeed some of them are already more advanced in North America than in this country. How are we to respond to such changes? How, in particular, are we to respond to the disparagement of moral earnestness? Are we to regard strict moral rules as no longer called for? What if they are increasingly replaced by patterns of behaviour geared to the promotion of indiscriminate consumption, the model citizen being someone who substitutes conspicuous spending for personal achievement and is uninterested in any other standard than monetary cost? It is impossible to isolate the moral trend from the social trend; they must be considered as parts of a complex.

One possible response is a wholehearted acceptance of this development. The unthinking are only too likely to drift into accepting it. And they will be cheered on by those who stand to gain most from it, financially or in terms of power and prestige. These are the people who may quietly devise our way of life, mould our attitudes, set the fashions which will replace stable values. (An unexpected outcome for the highminded liberal revolution of the nineteenth century!) And we who do think might be glad to be rid of the old restrictions on our efforts to find happiness in ways that do not obviously harm our neighbours, glad of the enlarged sympathy for the unprivileged, the young and the maladjusted, and the increased tendency to transfer their burdens to society as a whole. We might consider the enhanced comfort for all well worth the sacrifice of individual pride and independence, and of the old emphasis on moral integrity. So we might cheerfully look forward to a new society in which the tendencies discussed in these pages would be carried still further.

We can imagine that in such a society the issue between chastity and sexual freedom would be settled in favour of freedom, pre-marital sexual experiment would be normal, adultery a triviality, and change of partner no more serious than change of job. The logical outcome of this might well be the disappearance of marriage save between those who positively desired children and as much family life as the new society would allow. Fresh techniques of contraception would limit parenthood to the genuine enthusiasts, and with the development of eugenics even these might find themselves submitted to a screening process before they were permitted to breed. Titillation of the sexual impulse in entertainment and advertising might be regarded as a justifiable attempt to provide heightened experience for the many who lack other means of self-expression. Those who distinguish between "lower" and "higher" pleasures disregard the fact that there exist people for whom the "lower" pleasures are the only possible creative activities, the only foci of intense and conscious feeling, the only aesthetic outlets. As to family life, in the fully developed Permissive Society, two options present themselves. One is a form of specialization in which well-equipped enthusiasts with their assistants would rear large families including foster children. The other is a progressive weakening of family ties such as that envisaged by Young in *The Rise of the Meritocracy* so that the brighter children and perhaps all children would spend few of their working hours under the family roof but would do their homework and pursue their hobbies in school and in holiday camps. Psychiatrists would take over from the penal system the task of adjusting malcontents to social conformity with this design. Indignation against vice would give way to the reconstruction of disordered personalities. Everyday stresses would be relieved by medication. A society of the utmost blandness would ensue. If the commercial tycoons eventually proved unable to organize such a society, the general trend should be sufficiently set for a socialist élite to replace them without noticeable difference in daily living for the great majority. Then decisions about what was to be produced, and by what methods, how it should be distributed, who should occupy what job and under what conditions, would be made for all by top managers turned civil servants. Training, job, meals, living quarters, medical attention and recreation, would be provided by a single public organization so that the ordinary fellow need not worry about these things but could give all his attention when off duty to amusing himself. Advertising would be easily transformed into state propaganda. Individual protest would be ignored unless it became persistent, when it could be treated as symptomatic of an illness to be cured at public expense. If a man proved a reliable worker and socially amenable only when under the influence of appropriate drugs, then drugged he would be. Training-in of suitable attitudes would be undertaken first at school and later on the job. All of this is the logical outcome of the morally permissive trend; if the ordinary person is to be relieved of responsibility, some few persons in authority must undertake it on his behalf. Thus the need for individual conscience and individual moral struggle would disappear. And so the management's idea of the greatest happiness of the greatest number could be economically dispensed through the community.

Many people, however, are affronted when faced with so uncompromising a statement of the character of the fully developed Permissive Society in which individual moral choice is replaced by social conditioning. Bitter opposition might be expected from all those who considered that their roles in it did not compensate them for their loss of independence. Protest might take the non-political form of greatly increased general delinquency, as perhaps it already does in our younger age groups who are affected by boredom and frustration rather than by poverty. Who indeed wants to be a super-machine tending machines of lower complexity? It may after all be more satisfying to make one's own mistakes, endure one's own stresses and distresses, remain a rather uncomfortable but independent agent, in a word live one's own life. This seems to be the conclusion drawn by some of our young delinquents.

It is certainly the conclusion drawn by the more sophisticated group of the atheistic existentialists. Sartre, Camus and their followers, beginning from the position of religious and ethical scepticism, accept the decay of those assured "moral truths" by which older generations lived. For them, God is dead and everything is permitted. They believe that it is then up to individuals to invent values for themselves and live them; only thus can they become authentic beings. Any other course is one of *mauvaise foi*. This is the anguish and glory of the human condition, that men must perceive that they are nothing until they have created themselves through moral choice confirmed by action. They must decide their own ways of life, their own good and evil; copying or conforming is not valid. And the choice must be arbitrary, depending on men's own free volitions; it can be justified by nothing outside themselves. So the existentialist will always challenge political management and deny its claims to lay down the boundaries of good and evil for its subjects.

But to us it seems that the existentialist attempt to fashion and live by private moralities can succeed only through a feat of *mauvaise foi* as glaring as that of the moral conventionalist. For one cannot confer genuine worth and justification on a manner of living simply by plumping for it, even to the accompaniment of sweat and tears. One cannot make one experience yield greater satisfaction than another simply by saying to oneself that it shall be so. One has first to taste the experiences honestly and inquiringly; it is only thus that those which exhilarate or content more frequently than they disappoint will be discovered. Only the known quality of the experience itself can produce a justification which is more than a pretence. The existentialist attitude does indeed provide opposition to managers and manipulators. But its tendency is to fragment that opposition by emphasizing in each man his separateness from all the rest and by discouraging the pursuit of commonly acceptable ends and values.

The movement towards collective action, the dominance of the big organizations, is too powerful to be much embarrassed by individual acts of rejection. We cannot halt or evade it. Our problem is to humanize it.

Thus we cannot accept either of these moral standpoints, uncritical acceptance of the permissive morality or arbitrary revolt against it. We find the weakness of this morality where the existentialists find it. It encourages sloppy living, and in this there is inadequate satisfaction. Man is adapted to a life of ceaseless struggle against an unfriendly environment. When the environment becomes too bland, offers too little resistance, he is at a loss to get satisfaction out of life. For most of our genuine satisfactions are not those deliberately sought in the pursuit of love, fame or fine flavour; they are by-products of our moderate successes in the battle to adjust ourselves to people and circumstances. When we feel that on the whole we are not managing too badly, we experience a glow of satisfaction. Make the adjustment too easy and the glow dies down. The moments one looks back to with most pleasure, the vindicating moments of life, include many in which one's powers have been taxed to the utmost, and one has been doing something with full attention and all of one's ability . . . a difficult rock climb, the solution of a problem, the contemplation of a work of art in those favoured moments when one feels one has achieved communication with it, or the best hours of a love relationship. Thus an essential element in a satisfying life is self-respect, which comes from having done one's best, having lived up to standards which one thoughtfully and seriously accepts. It is only in this way that life can be justified despite its pains and disappointments. To think well of myself for having a bigger car or refrigerator than my friends is all very well while it lasts, but it vanishes as soon as one of them goes one better. But the satisfaction of having done what I thought right can last for life and depends on nobody but myself. It is, too, only on the basis of firm standards of values that one can respect and appreciate other people and other achievements. Thus the moral ideal we affirm is one which puts emphasis on self-discipline and acceptance of standards, and the social system we hope for is one which provides encouragement and opportunity for these things. The Permissive Society treats us all as capricious children, whereas what we need for a life worth living is to be encouraged to grow into full adults.

What are these standards to be? They cannot be the rigid Victorian rules which lingered into our grandparents' time. They will need to be more flexible in this rapidly changing age, putting more emphasis on the spirit and less on the letter. But we must look for a moral code designed for the self-respecting and responsible person trying to live on his own highest level of achievement and awareness.

In sexual morality we hope to see sex regarded as ideally an element in an intimate personal relationship of love and trust, to be approved of only when it conduces to such a relationship. In a serious and responsible view of sex one would be tolerant of sexual relations between young people not yet married but contemplating marriage, or between those in love but for some reason unable to marry. One would be intolerant of promiscuity, of sex indulged in merely for kicks or for experiment or for gain, and of any adulterous *affaire* which impaired an existing relationship of love and trust between spouses. One would, other things being equal, prefer the dissolution of a marriage lacking love and trust to its continuance.

In this matter, fiction exerts a substantial influence in conveying to young people their picture of what life is like and what conduct is normal and desirable. Victorian fiction did a great deal to promulgate the romantic ideal of lifelong affection based on youthful attraction, and managed to convince many young people of the plainly false proposition that the state of being in love is both a necessary and a sufficient condition for happy married life. Contemporary fiction for its part is doing much to disrupt what remains of our sexual morality by giving the impression that the only people worth writing about are sexually loose and casual. It would be humbug to blame only the mass media or the yellow Press for this; the fashion was introduced and is maintained by gifted writers who take their vocation seriously and claim credit for "realism".

As to the upbringing of children, the heart of the matter seems to be the diminished power and prestige of parents, especially fathers. If there is ground for suspicion that many children today are not being given sufficiently clear and firm moral guidance, and are being led to expect too much of life, the chief remedies are likely to be found in restoring some of the lost prestige and authority of parents. For all the evidence to hand suggests that when one tries to dispense with the family and have children brought up *en masse* by professionals, results are unsatisfactory. Restoring parental authority is not easy under present conditions. It might help if parents were more closely associated with school-teachers and more involved with the moral instruction that they give, instead of handing over their children to an alien authority whose ways they imperfectly understand and whose teaching may contradict their own. It might also help if the parents of juvenile delinquents were held directly responsible for the consequences of their children's misdeeds. Plainly it is desirable that mothers of young children should stay at home and care for them instead of going out to work, though it is difficult to see how they could best be induced to do this. Most important of all is that parents should be aware of their own standards as displayed by their conduct and of their own status and duties as upholders of those standards.

As regards crime, we are invited by the new outlook, first to accept psychological treatment alongside or instead of punishment as a way of dealing with offenders, and second to extend the plea of irresponsibility from cases of evident insanity to all kinds of mental abnormality, and perhaps in the end to dispense with the notion of criminal responsibility altogether. To the first proposal there can be no reasonable objection if the psychiatrists' methods show results: punishment is not so conspicuously effective that we can afford to turn down psychiatric help. But so far, it does not appear that psychiatry can cure any very high proportion of criminals. Probably the way offenders are dealt with makes rather little difference to the prevalence of crime. Opportunities and temptations to offend, the unlikeliness of being caught, the attitude to crime of the general public, are very likely more important factors; and, for the individual, what happens to him when he comes out of prison may matter more than what is done to him inside. There is reason to suspect that the general attitude to crime has changed in our generation; that offences against the law are regarded more as a matter of course, with greater indulgence or indifference. (Notice for instance how rarely nowadays bystanders will assist the police.) It is for this reason that we are unwilling to accept the second element of the new attitude to crime, the whittling away of the idea of criminal responsibility. We prefer the old-fashioned notion that breaches of the moral law and the law of the land are normally avoidable by anyone who thinks it worth his while to try, and that the responsibility for failure rests with the offender and not with society. Whatever penalties or treatments may be thought appropriate, a man is guilty of his intentional misdeeds, and this principle needs to be stoutly maintained to keep men sensible of their obligations to the law. While we are ready to trust judges with the power to punish those who defy the law, we are not so ready to trust any body of Straighteners with power to remake the characters of their fellow citizens in accordance with their own ideas.

But it is probably the economic order which is crucial in setting the pattern of our lives and attitudes. And here it is clear that, however much we value liberty, economic liberalism is an out-of-date creed. It is impossible to restore to the freelance craftsman or professional or to the small independent entrepreneur their one-time importance in the economy. And it is certainly not desirable to undo what has been done by way of collective provision for individual misfortunes. We need the Welfare State. Now the Welfare State will only work if there is a high degree of organization from the top, if industrial production and labour conditions are planned on a large scale and if social services are devised centrally and administered in gross . . . if in fact many formerly individual decisions are taken out of individual hands. At the same time, as the citizens come to depend more and more on collective action, and find corporations replacing individuals as employers and providers of services, there is increased need for a strong sense of obligation and loyalty to be cultivated towards these corporations and towards the community at large. But while the ordinary citizen comes to occupy a less responsible position in the management of affairs, his sense of moral responsibility grows weaker rather than stronger. The irresponsible attitude we have been describing is that of groups of people released from the pressure of harsh discipline, but as yet without much standing in society. Economic responsibility may be sought in two ways. In consumption, it is important that a man should have a range of choice, and that he should be able to spend his money in accordance with his own tastes and judgement of quality, unhampered either by overstandardization or by the misrepresentation and covert emotional influence of advertisements. Here socialism may offer us a release from the obsession with competitive acquisition which still dominates us. Here also the consumers' associations for testing and reporting on goods offered for sale, and for expressing to manufacturers the felt requirements of their customers, do help consumers to make their buying more rational and more expressive of their real needs. Yet more important, in production it matters for the development of a man's self-respect that he should be in some measure responsible, individually or in a small group, for the quality of the work he does, that there should be some performance or product that is recognizably his or his group's work, in which he can take some pride, and that work of high quality should gain him recognition in money or reputation. It is important too that he should know the function of the work he is engaged in and be able to regard it as a worthwhile contribution to his community's well-being. So it seems to us that the chief way to encourage the sense of moral responsibility, the acceptance of self-discipline, the willing adherence to standards, is to give everyone something of importance to do on his own and recognition for having done it. In order to prevent the development of the permissive society we are already engaged in building into something closely resembling Huxley's Brave New World we shall have to foster self-respect through individual responsibility.

# Index